I0024209

William A. Ogden

Highest Praise for Sabbath Schools

William A. Ogden

Highest Praise for Sabbath Schools

ISBN/EAN: 9783743330153

Manufactured in Europe, USA, Canada, Australia, Japa

Cover: Foto ©Thomas Meinert / pixelio.de

Manufactured and distributed by brebook publishing software (www.brebook.com)

William A. Ogden

Highest Praise for Sabbath Schools

Highest Praise

by W. A. Ogden

for Sabbath Schools

The Biglow & Main Company

NEW YORK and CHICAGO

F-46112

Og2h

HIGHEST PRAISE

FOR

SABBATH SCHOOLS.

EDITED AND COMPILED BY

W. A. OGDEN.

THE BIGLOW & MAIN CO.

76 EAST NINTH ST., NEW YORK.   215 WABASH AVE., CHICAGO.

MAY BE ORDERED THROUGH BOOKSELLERS AND MUSIC DEALERS.

[Copyright, 1895, by THE BIGLOW & MAIN CO.]

All Rights Reserved.

PREFACE.

N this Volume will be found an unusually large number of entirely NEW SACRED SONGS especially adapted to the wants of SABBATH SCHOOLS and YOUNG PEOPLE'S SOCIETIES.

The music is bright and sparkling, such as young people love to sing. The words have been carefully written and selected, so as to supply the ever increasing demand for NEW HYMNS suitable for use in connection with the varying subjects of the International Sabbath School Lessons.

The author of "HIGHEST PRAISE" is one of the most popular composers of Sabbath Schools Songs of the day, and has had the valuable assistance of IRA D. SANKEY and FANNY J. CROSBY in the selection of the Hymns.

Hoping that these new songs may help to swell the notes of Highest Praise unto Him "from Whom all blessings flow," we send them forth on their joyful mission.

NOTE: Nearly all the pieces in the *Collection are copyright in the United States and Great Britain, and neither words nor music can be reprinted in other country without the written permission of the owner of the copyright.*

THE BIGLOW & MAIN CO. PUBLISHERS

Highest Praise

FOR

Sabbath Schools.

WE BLESS HIS NAME.

W. A. O.

W. A. OGDEN.

1. In Highest Praise our songs we sing To Jesus Christ, our Lord and King, Who came e - ter - nal
2. In Highest Praise we bless His name, Who to the earth from glo - ry came, A world of sin - ners
3. In Highest Praise His name we bless, Who is our per-fect righteous-ness; May ev - 'ry tongue His
4. In Highest Praise may we a - dore His ho - ly name for - ev - er-more, With all the ransomed

FINE. DUET.   CHORUS.   D.S.

life to bring, And tri-umph o'er the grave, And tri-umph o'er the grave,
to re-claim, And free sal - va-tion bring, And free sal - va-tion bring,
name confess, And crown Him Lord of all, And crown Him Lord of all,
gone be-fore, In ev - er - last-ing bliss, In ev - er - last-ing bliss,

Copyright, 1895, by The Biglow & Main Co.

GRACIOUS HEAVENLY FATHER.

Rev. E. A. HOFFMAN.

W. A. OGDEN.

1. Gracious Heavenly Fath - er, Once a - gain we gath - er, From our homes so low - ly,
2. As we come be - fore Thee, Wor-ship-ful a - dore Thee, Con - de - scend to - ward us,
3. Glad-ly we will praise Thee, Grate-ful anthems raise Thee, Pa - tient Thou hast sought us.

To Thy courts so ho - ly; Hum-bly here we ten - der, For Thy love so ten - der,
And with peace re - ward us; Our pe - ti - tion hear - ing, And our spir - its cheer - ing.
With Thy blood hast bought us; Therefore we a - dore Thee, Humbly come be - fore Thee.

Prais - es, prais - es to Thy ho - ly name.
As we laud and bless Thy ho - ly name.
Now to mag - ni - fy Thy ho - ly name,

To be used after last stanza

MEN.

Copyright, 1894, by The Biglow & Main Co.

LET US DRAW STILL NEARER.

Mrs. C. L. Shaklock.

S. W. Straub.

1. Let us come to-day with sing-ing; To the house of pray'r and praise, Lov-ing
2. Near-er to the fount of mer-cy, Near-er to the Lord in pray'r; We shall
3. If to sweet the earth-ly meet-ing, In the tem-ple that we love; Oh how

hearts to Je-sus bring-ing, And a joy-ful song up-raise.
find His grace suf-fi-cient, We shall find acceptance there.
blest will be the greet-ing, In our Fa-ther's house a-bove.

Chorus.

Let us draw . . . still nearer,
Let us draw

To the Lord to-day; Then we'll see with vi-sion clear-er, How He guides us on the way.
blessed Lord

6

IN THY NAME.

FANNY J. CROSBY.   JAMES L. ORR.

1. In Thy name and not our own,   Lord we come be-fore Thy throne;   May our pray'rs to-geth-er rise, Borne like in-cense to the skies.
2. While Thy Ho-ly Word we read,   Help us all,   May its coun-sels guide our feet, Ear-ly to the mer-cy seat.
3. While our cheer-ful songs we raise,   Tune our grate-ful hearts to praise;   In o-be-dient love to Thee, May we all u-nit-ed be.
4. In the book of life di-vine,   May our names for-ev-er shine;   With the ran-somed may we stand, Robed and crowned at Thy right hand.

Chorus.

Bend to us Thy gra-cious ear, Bless our school and Teach-ers dear, Sa-cred may these moments be, Con-se-crat-ed Lord, to Thee.

Copyright 18.., by The Biglow & Main Co.

LOYAL UNTO JESUS.

BERTHA M. SCHWEIZER.

W. A. OGDEN.

1. Ev - er true and faith - ful, Un - to Christ, our King; We His loy - al
2. He is our Com - mand - er! In His name we go; On - ward, to the
3. Sound a - loud the trum - pet, Wave the ban - ner high: "For - ward" is the
4. Clad in gos - pel ar - mor, Bold - ly march a - long, Step by step al -

Chorus.

Loy - al un - to Je - sus,

Now His prais - es sing,
On to meet the foe,
Sig - nal - ed from the sky.
To the vic - tor's song.

sol - diers,
bat - tle,
watch - word
van - quish - ing

Well He car - eth for us, Sup - ply - ing all our needs,

Marching where He leads;

8

CONFESSING CHRIST.

E. E. HEWITT.

JNO. R. SWENEY.

1. Are we wit-nessing for Je - sus? With the prayer-ful, kind - ly word, Tell - ing humbly,
2. Are we wit-nessing for Je - sus? Stand-ing ev - er for His cause, Brave-ly own-ing
3. Are we wit-nessing for Je - sus? Do our lives His words o - bey? Prov - ing that His
4. Are we wit-ness-ing for Je - sus? In the hour of grief and pain, Can we point to

tell-ing tru - ly of the goodness of the Lord.
our al - legiance To His kingdom's ho - ly laws.
grace a - bounding, Keeps us while we trust and pray.
heavenly sunbeams, Shin-ing soft - ly through the rain?

Chorus.

Who - so - ev - er Me con-fess-eth, Saith the

Master whom we love. Him will I con - fess in glo - ry, At the Father's throne a - bove.

Copyright, 1891, by Jno. R. Sweney. Used by per.

UPON THE CROSS OF CALVARY.

Rev. E. A. HOFFMAN.

W. A. OGDEN.

1. Up - on the cross of Cal - va - ry The Sav - iour shed His blood, To res - cue me, and
2. My ma - ny sins He meek - ly bore, He bore, Up - on His guiltless head, When on the cross of
3. And now redeemed,this soul of mine, From con - dem - na - tion free. Re - joic - es in the

Chorus.

res - on - cited My wand - 'ring soul to God. } Yes, Je - sus died for me, To
Cal - va - ry His pre - cious blood was shed, }
bless - ed truth, That Je - sus died for me. }

for me.

Him all glo - ry be; In pa - tient un - com-plain-ing love, He gave Himself for me.

Copyright, 1896, by The Bigelow & Main Co.

10 IN THE NAME OF CHRIST.

W. A. OGDEN.

CHAS. K. LANGLEY.

FINE.

1. In the name of Christ, With our flag unfurled, We are march-ing on To sub-due the world;
2. In the name of Christ, In His glorious might, We will for-ward march In the ho-ly fight;
3. In the name of Christ, When the work is done, When the bat-tles fought, And the vic-t'ry won,

To the cross of Christ Ev'ry foe we'd bring, And the vic-to-ry glad-ly sing.
In His bless-ed name We will meet the foe, And to vic-to-ry on-ward go.
We will pass from earth To our home a-bove, Thro' the mer-it of Je-sus' love.

Chorus.

D. S.—To the cross of Christ Ev'ry foe we'd bring, And the vic-to-ry glad-ly sing.

Marching on with ban-ner bright, 'Gainst the foe and for the right.
Marching on with waving banner bright, 'Gainst the foe and for the right.

han-ner bright,

Copyright, 1894, by The Biglow & Main Co.

HEAR THEM TO-DAY.

FANNY J. CROSBY

W. A. OGDEN

1. Hear ye the song in the house of pray'r, Hear ye the sto - ry sweet;
2. Lis - ten, the cho - rus a - gain we hear, Breath-ing a Sav-iour's love;
3. Beau - ti - ful home where the chil - dren learn How to be good and kind;
4. Yes, we will come and our hearts we'll give, Je - sus, our Lord, to Thee;

Chil-dren have we
How can we
Now to its
Help us each

gath-ered to wor-ship there, Low at the Saviour's feet,
lin - ger when tones so dear, Tell us of joys a - bove,
por - tals we glad - ly turn, Je - sus, our Lord, to find,
mo-ment, for Thee to live, Hap - py we then shall be.

Chorus.

Hear them to-day, ten-der-ly say, —

"Come to the Sunday-school a-way!" Hear them to-day, ten-der-ly say, — "Come to the Sunday-school away!"

Copyright, 1893, by The Biglow & Main

11

ONWARD AND UPWARD.

Rev. JOHN O. FOSTER, arr

A. L. STOUGH.

1. On - ward the chil-dren are march - ing, On - ward and up-ward to - day; See how the
2. On - ward the chil-dren are march - ing, Joy free - ly blend-ing with cheers, Bright on the
3. On - ward the chil-dren are march - ing, Glad - ly their off'rings they bring; Help - ing the
4. God bless the ar - my of chil - dren Swell-ing the ranks of the brave; Hear them pro-

ranks of the loved ones Swell as they're marching a - way.
folds of their ban - ner, On-ward their motto ap - pears.
cause of the Mas - ter, While of His good-ness they sing.
claim-ing the til - ings, Je - sus is 'mighty - to save.

Chorus.

March - - ing, march - - ing, March - - ing, march - ing.

March - ing onward, marching upward.

March - ing, march - ing, The chil-dren are marching to-day.

March-ing on-ward, marching on.

March-ing a - way.

they're marching,

Copyright, 1895, by The Biglow & Main Co.

DAILY DUTIES.

BERTHA M. SCHWEIZER.

W. A. OGDEN

13

1. When thy hand its du-ty find-eth, La-bor thou with all thy might: Do not wait for great en-
2. If thy heart is full of sun-shine, Do not keep it all with-in: Shed its rays in lov-ing
3. Give thy strength to aid the wea - ry Who have ful-fil-len by the way. Point them to the path that
4. Fast thy bark of life is drift-ing On-ward to the oth-er shore. Therefore leave not for the

deav - ors, Do the lit - tle things in sight.
act - ions, Wea-ry souls for Christ to win.
lead - eth Up-ward, to the realms of day.
mor - row That which thou canst do be - fore.

Refrain.

O wait . . . not for the mor - row, But
Wait not for the mor - row,

cres.

speak the word to - day, That giv - eth peace and com-fort, That bright-ens all the way.

Copyright 18??, by The Bigelow & Main Co.

BRIGHT GLORY LAND!

IDA G. TREMAINE.

HUBERT P. MAIN.

1. There is a land beyond the stars, Glo-ry Land, bright Glory Land! Beyond the sunset's crimson bars,
2. The cit-y of our God is there, Glo-ry Land, bright Glory Land! Its jas-per walls with beauty fair,
3. We lift our eyes by faith, and see, Glo-ry Land, bright Glory Land! Where Christ Himself the light shall be,

Glo-ry Land, bright Glo-ry Land! A land of peace with-out al-loy; Of joy be-yond all
Glo-ry Land, bright Glo-ry Land! Its gates of pearl like sil-ver gleam, Its skies with fade-less
Glo-ry Land, bright Glo-ry Land! The songs of praise glad hearts shall sing; The ra-diant air with

earth-ly joy; And naught its calm can e'er de-stroy,— Glo - ry Land, bright Glo - ry Land!
sun-light beam, And thro' it rolls life's crys - tal stream, Glo - ry Land, bright Glo - ry Land!
mu - sic ring; Each voice pro-claim our Sav - iour, King, Glo - ry Land, bright Glo - ry Land!

Copyright, 1894, by The Biglow & Main Co. Used by per.

HEAR US, O SAVIOUR.

CHARLES BRUCE.

IRA D. SANKEY.

15

1. Hear us, O Sav-iour, while we pray, Hum-bly our need con-fess-ing; Grant us the
2. Know-ing Thy love, on Thee we call, Bold-ly Thy throne ad-dress-ing; Plead-ing that
3. Trust-ing Thy word that can-not fail, Mas-ter, we claim Thy prom-ise; Oh, that our

Refrain.

prom-ised show'rs to-day, Send them up-on us; O Lord,
show'rs of grace may fall,— Send them up-on us; O Lord,
faith may now pre-vail,— Send us the show-ers O Lord,

Send show'rs of bless-ing.

Send show'rs re-fresh-ing; Send us show'rs of bless-ing. Send them, Lord, we pray.

Copyright 1891 by Ira D. Sankey. Used by per.

16

ARISE, AND FOLLOW ME!

W. P. M.

WILLARD P. MORRIS.

1. The Mas-ter is come and call - eth, O broth-er He calls for thee; In ten-der-est
2. If thou wilt be-lieve Him ful - ly, That He is the Christ in - deed; He'll give to thee
3. Then trust Him and brave-ly fol - low The Sav-iour is kind and true; O serve Him with

tones He's say - ing "A - rise and fol - low Me;" "A - rise . . a - rise . . a -
life e - ter - nal, In this thy time of need.
joy and glad - ness, He's call - ing now for you.

pp Chorus.

rise, a - rise, a-rise

A-rise, a - rise, a-rise

rise and fol - low Me;" The Mas - ter is gen - tly call - ing, "A - rise and fol-low Me."
fol-low Me;

Copyright, 1-0, by The Biglow & Main Co.

THE SURE FOUNDATION.

BERTHA M. SCHWEIZER.

.W. A. OGDEN

1 Take Christ for thy foun - da - tion, In build-ing up life's years; Up - on this Rock es -
2 Tho' storms may lash to fu - ry, The break-ers all a - round, Thy fort - ress stands se -
3 God's arm is round a - bout thee, To strengthen and to save; 'Twas He who still'd the
4 Safe in His kind - ly keep - ing He guards thee ev - er - more. Then trust Him, He will

Chorus.

tab - lished Thy soul need have no fears.
cure - ly, Up - on a stead-fast ground. } Firm on the "Rock of A - ges," And
temp - est, And calmed the surg - ing wave.
guide thee, To Ca-naan's peace-ful shore.

shad-owed by God's hand, Thro' ev - ry gale that may as-sail, Se - cure - ly thou shalt stand.

Copyright, 1895, by The Biglow & Main Co.

BENEATH THE CROSS OF JESUS.

REV. J. D. HERR, D.D.

R. S. HANNA.

1. Be-neath the cross of Je-sus, how with con-trite heart; While in His work most
2. Be-neath the cross of Je-sus, I come at His com-mand, And of-fer for His
3. Be-neath the cross of Je-sus, I'll strive to do His will, His prom-i-ses shall

pre-cious view, I glad-ly take a part.
Set-view, My head, my heart, and hand.
cheer me. While I my task ful-fill.

Chorus.

O sa-cred cross of Je-sus, That tells of dy-ing love, That tells of com-ing glo-ry, Of rest, and peace a-bove.

Copyright, 1893, by The Biglow & Main Co.

HIS JEWELS. (Primary.)

LAURA E. NEWELL.

W. A. OGDEN.

1. When He maketh up His jew - els, in His ten-der-ness di - vine,
2. Thro' the sunshine and the shad - ow, Lead Thy lit - tle ones, we pray;
3. Then at last with-in Thy king - dom, May we dwell with se we love.

Chorus.

be a - mong the num - ber, In His di - a - dem to shine;
path of peace, and du - ty, Ev - er in the per-fect way.
mansions o - ver Jor - dan, Waiting now for us a - bove.

Hear Thy lit-tle-ones, O Sav-iour,

In Thy mer-cy now, we pray; May we shine among Thy Jew-els, In the great e-ter-nal day.

Copyright, 1893, by The Biglow & Main Co.

COME LET US WORSHIP.

W. A. O.

Geo. C. Hugg.

1. Come let us wor-ship, wor-ship and a-dore Him, He is the Lord, and we His chil-dren are;
2. Come let us wor-ship, doubting not, nor fear-ing, He will not scorn the grate-ful songs we sing;
3. Come let us wor-ship, praise and ad - o - ra - tion, Ev - er becomes the chil-dren of His grace:

Bow at His feet, and hum-bly there before Him, Of - fer with joy our praise and pray'r.
If in our hearts we watch for His ap-pear-ing, He will ac-cept the praise we bring.
Trust-ing a - lone in Him for full sal - va - tion, We shall be-hold the Fa - ther's face.

Chorus.

Come let us wor-ship, wor-ship the Lord, Ful - ly re - ly - ing on His blessed word,

Copyright, 1895, by The Bigelow & Main Co.

COME LET US WORSHIP.—Concluded.

Come let us wor-ship, bow-ing down be-fore Him. He is our God, and He is a - lone.

OUTSIDE THE FOLD.

Edw. Willet

MARION E. OGDEN

1. Weak and sin - ful tho' we are, This glo-rious hope we hold, D. S. Je-sus will not
2. Tho' we oft - en lose our way, In dark-est night and cold, D. S. Je-sus will not
3. He will save us from our sin. And all its dread a-larms, D. S. He will keep us

FINE.

Out - side the fold. Out - side the fold.
Out - side the fold. Out - side the fold.
Safe in His arms, Safe in His arms,

leave His Lambs out - side the fold.
let us stay Out - side the fold.
safe with - in His lov - ing arms.

D. S.

Copyright, 1905, by The Rodeheaver Co.

O COME TO JESUS TO-DAY.

LAVILLE D. LANDON.

FRANK J. ROBERTSON.

1. O soul cast down, and wea - ry, With bur-dens sore op - prest, Come rest
2. O soul op-prest with an - guish, Thy peace thou'lt nev-er find, Un - til
3. A ref - uge sure, a - bid - ing, In Je - sus thou shalt know, When to

in lov - ing
thou seek-est
His lov - ing

Chorus.

faith to - day Up - on the Sav-iour's breast.
it by faith, In Christ, the Sav-iour kind.
arms in faith Be - liev - ing thou shalt go.

O come, O come, O come, O come, O come to

Je - sus to - day; All ye that are wea - ry, With burdens op-prest, O come to Je-sus to - day.

Copyright, 1895, by The Biglow & Main Co.

BLESSED IS HE.

W. A. Ogden.

W. A. O.

1. When to Je - ru - sa - lem He came, The chil-dren sweet-ly sang; Ho-san - na to the
2. They-spread their gar-ments in His way, To hon - or Him, their King; But we would great-er
3. We wel-come Thee, O bless-ed Lord, Here in Thy courts be - low, And pray that all who

Chorus.

Sav-iour's name, And loud their voi-ces rang. } "Ho-san - na! Ho-san - na! Oh,
hom - age pay, — Our hearts to Him we'd bring. } "Bless-ed is He, bless-ed is He!"
gath - er here, Thy sav - ing grace may know. }

bear the joy-ful word, "Ho-san-na! bless-ed is He that cometh In the name of the Lord!"

Copyright, 1895, by The Biglow & Main Co.

24

PILGRIMS ON THE WAY. (Primary.)

MARY P. COLLINS, arr.

A. B. KAUFFMAN.

1. We are lit-tle pil-grims In the nar-row way. Marching on to-geth-er
2. In the dew-y morn-ing, In the noon-day fair, We will fol-low Je-sus,
3. In the up-per king-dom Lit-tle pil-grims wear Robes of snow-y white-ness,

To a bright-er day; Seek-ing for the glo-ry Which the soul a-waits,
And His ban-ner bear; Trust-ing in His prom-ise, We will jour-ney on,
Palms of vict-'ry bear; Cast their crowns of glo-ry Down at Je-sus' feet.

Chorus.

When the lit-tle wea-ry pil-grim Pass-es thro' the gates, We'll jour ney on, For
Till we reach the home in glo-ry, And our crowns have won,
Wea-ry hours are there for-got-ten, Hap-pi-ness com-plete. We'll journey on,

By per. of W. A. Ogden, owner of copyright.

PILGRIMS ON THE WAY.—Concluded.

Je - sus is our Guide. In the nar-row way we're passing To the oth - er side.

ARISE, AND COME TO JESUS!

WILLARD P. MORRIS.

Words arr.

1. A - rise, and come to Je - sus, He call-eth thee to - day: The bus - y crowd is
2. A - rise, and fol - low Je - sus, Where-ev - er He may lead: The' rough the path, and
3. His feet were torn and bleed - ing, Who passed this way be - fore; But now a King in

D.S.—God's ho - ly book is

Fine. **Chorus.**

thronging The broad and downward way }
thorn - y, Press on with all thy speed. } O come, O come, And on to glo - ry go.
glo - ry, He reign-eth ev - er - more. }

O come, O come,

up - on The way of life to shine.

Copyright, 1895, by The Biglow & Main Co.

AN OPEN BIBLE.

HENRY M. KING, D. D.

WM. J. KIRKPATRICK.

1. An o - pen Bi - ble for the world! May this our glo-rious mot - to be! On ev - ery
2. Wher-e'er it goes its gold - en light, Streaming as from an un-veiled sun. Shall dis - si -
3. It shows to men the Fa-ther's face, All ra - diant with for-giv - ing love; And to the
4. It tells of Je - sus and His death, Of life pro-cured for dy - ing men; And to each
5. It of - fers rest to wea - ry hearts; It com-forts those who sit in tears; To all who

breeze its flag un-furled Shall scat - ter bless-ings rich and free.
pate the clouds of night, I'n - do the work that sin has done.
lost of hum - ble faith, Pro-claims sweet mer - cy from a - bove.
soul of hum - ble faith, It son-ship gives with God a - gain.
faint it strength imparts; And gilds with hope the e-ter - nal years.

Chorus.

Blest word of God! . . . Blest word of God!

send forth thy light . . . O'er ev - ery land and ev - ery sea, and ev - er - y sea.

send forth thy light

Copyright, 1895, by Wm. J. Kirkpatrick. Used by per.

AN OPEN BIBLE—Concluded.

Till all who wan-der in the night Are led to God and heaven by thee.

COME, COME TO-DAY.

F. J. CROSBY.

W. P. MORRIS.

1. O hear the Sav-iour call-ing, In tones like mu-sic fall-ing, Why not o-bey;
2. In sim-ple faith be-liev-ing, His ten-der love re-ceiv-ing, Why not o-bey;
3. He's wait-ing at the foun-tain, That flows from yon-der mount-ain,—Why not o-bey;

He of-fers full sal-va-tion; Slight not His in - vi - ta-tion; Why not o-bey; Come, come to - day.
Thy man-y sins confessing, Thou shalt obtain His blessing; Why not o-bey; Come, come to - day.
O be His child for ev - er, And He will leave thee never; Why not o-bey; Come, come to - day.

Copyright, 1897, by The Bigelow & Main Co.

A CHILD OF JESUS.

IDA SCOTT TAYLOR.

W. A. OGDEN.

1. To do my du - ty day by day, In the name of the King of kings, I'll strive by faith, I'll
2. To speak a lov - ing word of cheer, In the name of the King of kings, Shall be my greatest
3. To guard my tongue from speaking ill, In the name of the King of kings, I'll try to do my
4. I'll strive some earn - est deed to do, In the name of the King of kings, To keep my spir - it

watch and pray, In the name of the King of kings, A child of Je - sus I would be, For
pleas - ure here, In the name of the King of kings, A child of Je - sus I would be, For
Mas - ter's will, In the name of the King of kings, A child of Je - sus I would be, For
ev - er true, In the name of the King of kings, A child of Je - sus I would be, For

FINE.

oh, He gave His life for me! I want to serve Him faith - ful - ly, And hon - or the King of kings.

D.S. — I want to serve Him faith ful ly, And hon or the King of kings.

Copyright 1896, by The Bigelow & Main Co.

A CHILD OF JESUS.—Concluded.

D. S.

Chorus.

And hon - or the King of kings, of kings, And hon - or the King of kings.

WHO IS THERE?

W. P. MORRS.

Words arr.

1. Knocking, knocking, who is there? Knocking, knocking, oh how fair! 'Tis the Sav-iour, wait-ing,
2. Knocking, knocking, lin-gers He. Waiting, wait-ing, pa-tient-ly, O my soul why still de-
3. Knocking, knocking, still He's there, Waiting, wait-ing, wond'rous fair, Not in vain, Lord, wilt Thou

plead-ing, At thy heart He's in - ter-ced-ing, O trou-bled soul, He can make thee whole
by Him? to my soul why cru - ci-fy Him, O doubt-ing heart, Let Him not de - part
beat-ing At my sin - ful heart en-treat-ing Tho' I'm un-clean Sav-iour en - ter in.

By per. of W. P. Ogden, owner of Copyright.

WE THANK THEE, LORD.

FANNY J. CROSBY.

WILLARD P. MORRIS.

1. We thank Thee Lord, that chil - dren, May on Thy name be - lieve; And if, in faith they
2. We thank Thee Lord, that chil - dren, Thy feast of love may share; The young-est one a -
3. We thank Thee for the prom - ise, That Thou art ev - er nigh; To aid us with Thy
4. And while Thy con - stant mer - cies, Like gold - en sunbeams fall; O may we love each

Chorus.

ask Thee, For - give-ness may re - ceive; We come, as Thou hast taught us, We
mong us, May find a wel-come there.
coun - sel, And guide us with Thine eye.
oth - er, And love Thee most of all.

lift our souls to Thee; With this the lan-guage of our hearts, "Dear Lord, remem-ber me."

Copyright, 1893, by The Biglow & Main Co.

WE'LL FOLLOW ON.

FANNY J. CROSBY.

CHAS. K. LANGLEY.

1. O hap-py ones, that sweet-ly sing, In yon-der world so fair: Your foot-prints
2. We'll sing of Him, our bless-ed Lord, Who had His glo-ry down; Who bore our
3. We fol-low on with trust-ing hearts, For o'er life's troubled way. The same pro-

Chorus.

on the sands of time, We're left to guide us there.) We'll fol-low on, still looking up, Pro-
sins up - on the cross, That we might we'ra crown }
tect-ing hand is ours, That led you, day by day. }

Where-by and by this grace di-vine, We'll meet and sing with you.
yond the oth-er blue,

I'VE LEARNED TO LOVE THE SAVIOUR.

W. A. O.

Rev. R. C WARD.

1. I've learned to love the Sav-iour, He did so much for me, That I'm constrained by His dy-ing
2. I've heard His ma-ny coun-sels, I've read His ho-ly word, And thro' me by His
3. When from the fold I wan-dered In sin-ful paths a-stray; He led
4. So now, I go re-joic-ing His ho-ly name to bear; And if I true and

grace di-vine His fol-l'wer now to be,
love for me, My soul with joy is stirr'd.
pre-cious truth, To seek the bet-ter way.
faith-ful prove, A crown of life I'll wear.

Chorus. *Bass obligato.*

O bless-ed, bless-ed Lord,

O bless-ed, bless-ed Lord.

O bless-ed, bless-ed Lord.

O dear and heav'nly Friend, support me by Thy grace di-vine, And keep me to the end.

dear and heav'nly Friend,

Copyright, 189-, by The Biglow & Main Co.

WALKING IN THE LIGHT.

Dr. J. J. MAXFIELD.

W. A. OGDEN.

1. Are you trust-ing ful-ly in the Lord, Are you keep-ing your ar-mor al-ways bright?
2. Is He more to you than aught be-side, E'en your sword and your buckler in the fight?
3. Let us gird our loins to run the race; Al-ways striv-ing the prize to keep in sight;

FINE.

Do you strive to gain the blest re-ward, By walk-ing with Je-sus in the Light?
In His ser-vice shall you e'er a-bide, Still walk-ing with Je-sus in the Light?
And the Lord will give us conq'ring grace, While walk-ing with Je-sus in the Light.

D.S.—Let us take our cross and jour-ney on, Still walk-ing with Je-sus in the Light.

Chorus.

In the Light, in the Light, Let us walk with Je-sus in the Light,
In the Light, in the ev-er blessed Light,

D.S.

Copyright 1896, by W. A. ...

I NEED THY CARE.

ARTHUR LINDEN.

FRANK J. ROBERTSON.

1. God, I need Thy ten-der care,— Thy hand to guide me day by day; Thy grace, my
2. I need Thee ev-'ry pass-ing hour; Thy ho-ly word my way to show; O may I
3. I shall not fal-ter in the way, If Thou, O Lord art by my side; Thy prom-is-
4. I need Thee when at last I come To cross the riv-er, dark and wide: Then Sav-iour,

dai-ly cross to bear, And keep me in the narrow way.
trust Thy saving pow'r, And all Thy loving kindness know.
es my heart shall stay, And in Thy love I shall a - bide.
bear my spir-it home To that fair land beyond the tide.

Chorus.

I need Thy care, I need Thy care,

Ev-'ry day I need Thy care; O leave me not alone, dear Saviour, For ev-'ry day I need Thy care.

Copyright, 1896, by The Biglow & Main Co.

WILL YOU REAP FOR THE MASTER?

Mrs. J. Wilson

Willard P. Morris.

1. Lift your eyes and be-hold yon-der white har-vest field, Stretching forth in the dis-tance a - way;
2. You can work nev - er-more when the night com-eth on, And the shad-ows of death round you fall;
3. In the har - vest for souls, will you reap for the Lord; Shall His pleading with you be in vain?

Fine.

Of un-speak-a - ble worth to the Lord is its yield, And He call-eth for reap-ers to - day.
Op - por-tu - ni - ty then will for - ev - er be gone; Has-ten now at the dear Master's call.
They who la - bor are prom-ised a pre-cious re-ward; Joy e - ter - nal, the reap-ers shall gain.

D. S.—har-vest is great, And the time speed-eth fast, Will you reap for the Mas-ter to - day?

D. S.

Will you reap . . . in the field? . . At His feet golden sheaves will you lay? Let the
Will you reap,
in the field?

Copyright, 1895, by The Biglow & Main Co.

I KNOW THAT MY REDEEMER.

FANNY J. CROSBY.

CHAS. K. LANGLEY.

1. Tho' here I see but dark - ly, And skies with clouds are dim; I'll trust my Saviour's
2. I know that ev - ery mo - ment He saves me by His grace; In what - so - e'er be-
3. I know that in His king - dom So bright and fair to see, There is, if I am

Chorus.

prom - ise, And leave my all to Him. } I know that my Re-deem - er Is watching
falls me, His lov - ing hand I trace. }
faith - ful, A home prepared for me. }

o - ver me; I know His arm of mer - cy Will my pro - tec - tion be.

Copyright, 1895, by The Bigelow & Main Co.

BLESSED WORDS.

FANNY J. CROSBY.

W. A. OGDEN.

1. In the land of an - cient sto - ry, Where the the palms their branches long; Of Mes - si - ah
2. Still they sung, and watched and wait-ed, Till their hearts grew weak and old; And they pass'd a -
3. O the glo - ry that de-scend-ed When the Son of God was born. And the hal - le -
4. He has come, the Lord's a - noint-ed; Ev - 'ry heart with rap-ture swells! Haste to wor-ship

Chorus.

and His com - ing, Ho - ly pro - phets lived and sung,
way, be - liev - ing Christ would come as was fore-told. }
In - jah cho - rus First proclaimed His na - tal morn. } Bless - ed words of con - so - la - tion,
and a - dore Him, Ring the mer - ry Christ-mas bells. }

Heal-ing balm for ev - 'ry na - tion, — Christ, the hope of our sal - va - tion, O - ver all shall reign.

HEAVENLY FATHER, GRANT THY BLESSING.

F. J. CROSBY.

H. P. DANKS.

1. Heav'n-ly Fa - ther, grant Thy blessing, Thro' Thy well - be - lov - ed Son; May Thy peace that pass-eth knowl-edge, Rest up - on us, ev - 'ry one; Let Thy word like seed be plant-ed In our youth-ful hearts, we pray; Bear-ing fruit that shall be gar-nered In the realms of end-less day.

2. Lov - ing Sav-iour, guide our footsteps In the path that we should go; May taught us, In our lives Thy praise to show; May the pre-cious, gold-en mo-ments, In Thy tem - ple spent with Thee, Lead us on to high-er du - ties, What-so-ev - er our cross may be.

3. Ho - ly Spir - it - gracious Teacher, Grant Thy presence ere we part; Keep our thoughts from sin-ful pleas-ures, Guard and com-fort ev - 'ry heart, Fa - ther, Son and Ho - ly Spir - it, God whom earth and heav'n a - dore; Be a-mong us dwell with-in us, Now, henceforth, and ev - er-more.

Copyright, 1896, by The Biglow & Main Co.

LOOK UP! LIFT UP!

W. A. OGDEN.

W. A. O.

1. Let the lamp of faith be burn - ing, Let its flame flash out o'er the wave; Bid the shipwreck'd
2. Lend a hand to lift them up - ward, Till their feet shall stand on the Rock; And they dwell in
3. Send the tid - ings o'er life's o - cean, Waft the song of joy far and near; Tell the help - less

soul look up - ward To Him who a - lone can save. } Look up! . . Lift up! . . The
faith se - cure - ly, Safe from the tem - pest's shock. } Look up! Lift up
all a - round you That soon will the morn ap - pear. }

Chorus.

soul from sin's dark wave, With earn - est, true en - deav - or, Lend a help - ing hand to save.

Copyright, 1891, The Ogden & Music Co.

CLEANSE MY HEART.

Clifford Trembly.

C. A. Shaw.

1. O may I walk with Thee, O Christ, My life be hid in Thine; And may I feel Thy
2. O may my heart be pure, O God, And free from ev-ery sin; And may Thy ho-ly
3. O may I live a ho-ly life, All e-vil ways to shun; That I may hear Thee

Chorus.

Sav-ing grace; Re-new this heart of mine, of mine. } Cleanse my heart, cleanse my heart, Cleanse and
love for aye A-bound its depths with-in, with-in. }
say at last, The blessed words "Well done; Well done."

keep it ev-er Thine; Bless-ed Lord, and Sav-iour mine, Cleanse my heart, and keep it Thine.

Copyright, 1895, by The Bigelow & Main Co.

ON, CHRISTIAN SOLDIER.

W. A. O.

W. A. OGDEN.

1. On, Chris-tian sol - dier, on to the con-flict, Now the strife be - gin, See all around you
2. Go to the wounded, tell them how glad-ly Christ would make them whole, How He hath of - fered
3. Speak to the dy - ing, point them to Je - sus, Words of com - fort give; Tell them the Saviour

Chorus.

comrades are ly - ing, Pierc'd by darts of sin.
mer - cy and par-don To the faint - ing soul. Save them, oh, save them to-day! Point them to
now will receive them, They may look and live.

Je - sus the Way; Bind up the hearts all brok - en around you; For the dy - ing, pray.

Copyright, 1895, by The Biglow & Main Co.

NEVER SAY GOOD-BYE.

F. J. CROSBY.

IRA D. SANKEY.

1. O bless - ed home where those who meet Shall nev - er say good - bye; Where kin - dred souls each oth - er greet, And nev - er say good - bye.

2. Be - yond this vale of toil and care. We'll nev - er say good - bye; We part in tears on earth, but there—We'll nev - er say good - bye.

3. When safe a - mong the ransom'd throng, We'll nev - er say good - bye; Where life is one e - ter - nal song, We'll nev - er say good - bye.

4. On yon - der fair and peace - ful shore, We'll nev - er say good - bye; But dwell with Christ for - ev - er - more, And nev - er say good - bye.

Chorus.

We'll nev - er say good - bye, . . We'll nev - er say good - bye; In that fair land be - yond the sky, We'll nev - er say good - bye.

Copyright, 1890, by The Biglow & Main Co

FRESH AS THE DEW.

W. A. O.

W. A. OGDEN

1. Fresh as the dew of morn - ing, Pure as the sun's bright rays, Ring out the chil-dren's
2. Sweet are the songs of an - gels, Pur - er the ransomed strain; Yet from the lips of
3. Still as of old. the chil-dren Sweet their ho-san - nas sing, Prais-ing the bless - ed

Chorus.

To the Re-deem-er's praise, "Glo - ry to God!" they're singing, Praise to the
voic - es chil-dren, Sound-eth a glad re - frain.
Sav - iour. Prais-ing the Lord, their King.

Lamb they're bring-ing, Glad are the voic - es ring - ing, Tuned to the notes a - bove.

Copyright, 1893, by The Biglow & Main Co.

THY DAILY WALK.

W. A. O.

W. A. OGDEN.

1. If thy walk is up-ward in the nar-row way That leads to the home in glo-ry,
2. If thine eyes are watch-ing for the Mas-ter's feet,—That trod in the way thou'rt go-ing,
3. If in love thou'rt walk-ing with the Sav-iour blest, With a heart that is true and faith-ful;

If thy path grows bright-er with the com-ing day,
If thine ears are list-'ning for His com-ing sol-sweet,
If thy soul is long-ing for the heav'n-ly rest.

Then all shall be well with thee.
Then all shall be well with thee.
Then all shall be well with thee.

Chorus.

Walk ... ing in the nar-row way, That leads to our rest in glo-...
Walking in the way, in the nar-row way.

THY DAILY WALK.—Concluded.

Sing-ing as we go from our home be - low, Tell-ing out the old, old, old. Sto - ry.

IN TIME OF NEED.

JULIA H. JOHNSTON.

ALFRED BEIRLY.

1. Fear not the track-less wil-der-ness, O wea-ry pil-grim, on-ward press; His word of promise
2. The tempters darts may oft as - sail; But hope and cour-age will not fail; Lift up thy heart, dis-
3. In storm, and darkness and dis-may, A hand di-vine will guide the way; Till Canaan's shore is

D.S.—Lift up thy heart, His

FINE. Refrain.

bold-ly plead, Who giv-eth help in time of need.) In time of need, in time of need.
miss thy fear, For One who loves thy soul, is near. }
won at last, And all thy "time of need" is past. } His promise true, sin - - cere-ly plead;

D.S.

prom-ise plead, Who giv-eth help in time of need.

Copyright, 1890, by A. Bierly. Used by per.

O BLESSED SAVIOUR.

Fanny J. Crosby.

Chas. Edw. Prior.

1. O blessed Sav-iour, Thine arms of love and mer-cy, Reach for Thy children when from Thee they stray;
2. O blessed Sav-iour, when weak and heavy heart-ed, Thou dost not leave us here to walk a - lone;
3. O blessed Sav-iour, the lessons Thou hast taught us. May we re-joic-ing, hon-or and o - bey;

When in-to dan-ger they rush with careless foot-steps, Blind to the per-il that be - set their way;
Still in com-pas-sion Thy lov-ing arms ex-tend-ed, Reach to en-fold us and pro-tect Thine own;
Help us to fol - low wher-ev-er du-ty calls us, Cheer with Thy presence and defend our way;

They hear Thy voice divine, that soft ly whispers them, And gen-tly calls them to Thy fold a - gain.
O Thou in whom we trust, our never-changing Friend, Be near, and help us till our days shall end.
Thou, Lord, a-lone canst save from every tempting snare, O guide us, guard us, and for heav'n pre-pare.

Copyright, 1893, by The Biglow & Main Co.

THE HIGHWAY OF OUR GOD.

IDA SCOTT TAYLOR.

W. A. OGDEN.

1. Let earth Jehovah's praise declare, And spread His fame abroad; And let the desert
2. Let vernal valleys clap their hands, Let woodland echoes ring; And herald thro' the
3. Let mountains, hills, and dales rejoice, And songs of rapture raise; And let old ocean's
4. He comes in majesty and might His kingdom to proclaim; Let all the sons of

Chorus.

isles prepare The highway of our God.
world abroad The coming of the King.
mighty voice Awake and sound His praise.
men unite, To magnify His name.

Prepare ye the way of the Lord! . . Pre-
Pre - pare ye the way,

pare ye the way of the Lord! Thro' all the desert isles abroad, Make straight the highway of our God.

Copyright, 1888, by The Biglow & Main Co.

THE KING'S INVITATION.

LIDIE H. EDMUNDS.

JNO. R. SWENEY.

1. Hark! a message from the King of glo - ry. Hear it ring-ing thro' the wide, wide world,
2. Emp-ty - ty-hand-ed, let us go to Je - sus, Take the gar-ment of His right-eous - ness;
3. In the pal-ace where His glo - ry shin-eth, He will gath-er ev-'ry blood-washed soul;

"Come ye sin - ners, poor and need - y;" See the ban - ner of the cross un-furled.
He has made a full pro - vis - ion, He is wil - ling to re - ceive and bless.
There we'll see Him in His beau - ty. While e - ter-nal hal - le - lu - jahs roll.

Chorus.

Who will ask for the wed-ding gar - ment, Of-fered free - ly in the Sav-iour's name?

Copyright, 1901, by Jno. R. Sweney. Used by per.

THE KING'S INVITATION.—Concluded.

Who will ac-cept the King's in-vi-ta-tion? Who'll be pres-ent at the sup-per of the Lamb?

WE ARE LITTLE TRAVELERS.

Wm. Stevenson.

Rev. R. Lowry.

1. We are lit-tle trav-lers, Marching, marching. We are lit-tle trav-lers, Marching on; Walking on;
2. We are lit-tle la-b'rers, Work-ing, work-ing. We are lit-tle la-b'rers, Work-ing on; Nev-er
3. We are lit-tle sol-diers, Fight-ing, fight-ing. We are lit-tle sol-diers, Fight-ing on; Warring
4. We are lit-tle pil-grims, Hop-ing, hop-ing. We are lit-tle pil-grims, Hop-ing on; For a

In the nar-row way, Shunning paths that lead a-stray. We are lit-tle trav-lers, Marching on.
I-dling time a-way, Bus-y work-ing ev-'ry day. We are lit-tle la-b'rers, Work-ing on.
'gainst the pow'r of sin. Foes with-out and foes with-in. We are lit-tle sol-diers, Fight-ing on.
coun-try bet-ter far. Where one crown and kingdom are, We are lit-tle pil-grims, Hop-ing on.

Copyright, 1877, by The Biglow & Main Co.

50

WINNING THE WORLD FOR JESUS.

IDA SCOTT TAYLOR.

W. A. OGDEN.

1. We're winning the world for Je - sus, Spreading a-broad His praise; Tell-ing the joys of His
2. We're winning the world for Je - sus, Tell - ing His boundless love; Making the bur-den of
3. We're winning the world for Je - sus, Seek - ing His name to praise; Striving to hon - or the

great sal - va - tion, Wak-ing the earth with His proc - la - ma - tion; Winning the world for
oth - ers light-er, Mak-ing their path-way each mo-ment bright-er; Winning the world for
Lord of glo - ry, Tell-ing His won-drous, and thrill-ing His sto - ry; Winning the world for

Chorus.

Je - sus, For Je - sus, the King di - vine.
Je - sus, For Je - sus, the King di - vine.
Je - sus, For Je - sus, the King di - vine.

Sav-iour we would faith - ful be,

Copyright, 1895, by The Biglow & Main Co.

WINNING THE WORLD FOR JESUS. Concluded.

Winning hearts and lives to Thee, Thro' Thy wondrous grace so free, Je-sus, our King di-vine.

HE WILL CARE FOR ME.

W. P. M.

WILLARD P. MORRIS.

1. When my heart is sore dis-trest, I will go to Je-sus; He will give me peace and rest,
2. When temp-ta-tion grieves me sore, I will go to Je-sus; For He will oft temp-ta-tion bore,
3. When I walk in paths of peace, I will go to Je-sus; For He will my joy in-crease,

D.S.—He will give me peace and rest.

FINE. Chorus.

He will care for me, He will care for me,
And will care for me, He will care for me,
He will care for me.

will care for me,

will care for me.

He will care for me.

He will care for me.

Copyright, 1895, by The Biglow & Main Co.

52

BELIEVE AND OBEY.

JULIA STERLING.

IRA D. SANKEY.

1. Press on-ward, press on-ward, and trusting the Lord,
Re-member the promise proclaim'd in His word:
2. Press on-ward, press on-ward, if you would secure
The rest of the faith-ful, a-bid-ing and sure;
3. Press on-ward, press on-ward, your courage re-new;
The prize is be-fore you, the crown is in view.

He guid-eth the footsteps, di-rect-eth the way
Of all who con-fess Him, believe, and o-bey.
The gift of sal-va-tion is of-fer'd to-day
To all who con-fess Him, believe, and o-bey.
His love is so boundless, He'll nev-er say nay
To those who con-fess Him, believe, and o-bey.

Chorus.

Be-lieve and o-bey, believe and o-bey; The Mas-ter is call-ing, no long-er de-lay:

Copyright, 1894, by The Biglow & Main Co.

BELIEVE AND OBEY.—Concluded.

The light of His mercy shines bright on the way Of all who confess Him, believe, and obey.

BLESSED DAY. A Sabbath Hymn.

F. J. CROSBY.

D. E. JONES.

1. Bless-ed day. when pure de-vo-tions Rise to God on wings of love;
2. Bless-ed day. when bells are call-ing Wea-ry souls from earth-ly care;
3. Bless-ed day. so calm and rest-ful Bring-ing joy and peace to all;
4. Bless-ed day. thy light is fad-ing One by one its beams de-part.

When we catch the dis-tant mu-sic Of the an-gel choirs a-bove,
And we come with hearts up-lift-ed To the ho-ly place of pray'r;
Lin-ger yet in tran-quil beau-ty Ere the shades of eve-ning fall,
May their calm sweet re-col-lec-tion Still a-bide in ev-ery heart.

Words Copyright 1896 by The Biglow & Main Co.

BEARING THE CROSS.

Eben E. Rexford.

W. A. Ogden.

1. When I am worn and wea - ry, And read - y to de - spair; I think of Thee, my Sav - iour.
2. When I would murmur, Sav - iour, Be - neath my small - er load, And faint - ing, weak and wea - ry,
3. What is my small - est bur - den To that my Sav - iour bore! Be still my heart, and murmur

And what Thou hadst to bear. Thy cross, a - las! how heav - y; So steep the ston - y way;
Sink down be - side the road,— Give me, dear Lord, a vis - ion Of rug - ged Cal - va - ry,
Be - neath thy load no more. Bear pa - tient - ly thy cross - es In ways the Mas - ter trod,

Chorus.

Dear Lord what is my bur - den, Compared with Thine, to - day; }
And then Thine own cross bearing, To help, and strengthen me. } O Christ, Thou burden - bear - er,
And fol - low in the foot - steps That lead thee up to God.

Copyright, 1895, by The Biglow & Main Co.

BEARING THE CROSS.—Concluded.

Thy foot-prints still I see; Oh help me now to fol-low And bear my cross for Thee.

JEWELS, PRECIOUS JEWELS. (Primary.)

LAURA E. NEWELL

D. W. CRIST.

1. Jew-els for Thy di-a-dem, Sav-iour we would be; Ev - er in Thy crown to shine.
2. Jew-els for Thy di-a-dem, Chil-dren tho' we are, We would help to send Thy word
3. Jew-els for Thy di-a-dem, Sav-iour, grant that we, When our life on earth is done.

D. S.—Yon-der in our home a - bove.

D. S.

First Chorus.

Lamb of Cal - va - ry,
Un - to lands a - far.
Still may shine for Thee.

Jew - els, pre - cious jew - els,   In Thy crown to shine.

Through Thy love di - vine.

Copyright, 1882, by D. W. Crist. Used by per.

56

BLESSED PEACE.

FANNY J. CROSBY.

WILLARD P. MORRIS.

1. Peace that makes my la - bor sweet, Peace that keeps me at Thy feet, Peace what - ev - er my
2. Peace when earth - ly friends are few, Peace when gath'ring storms I view, Peace in trust - ing
3. Peace in sick - ness or in health, Cloud, or sun - shine, want, or wealth, Peace in lov - ing
4. Peace that calms my throbbing breast, Gives me tran - quil, per - fect rest; Peace that on - ly

Refrain.

cares may be, Bless - ed
on - ly Thee, Bless - ed
Saviour, grant Thou me.
Saviour, grant Thou me.
comes from Thee, Bless - ed

Peace in sor - row, and in joy, Peace the

Saviour, grant Thou me.
Saviour, grant Thou me.

world can ne'er de - stroy, Peace that draws my soul to Thee, Bless - ed Saviour, grant Thou me.

Copyright, 1894, by The Biglow & Main Co.

THE DOOR IS OPEN.

FANNY J. CROSBY.

W. A. OGDEN.

1. The door is o-pen wea-ry one, The fount is flow-ing free: Go lay thy bur-den at the
2. The door is o-pen wand'ring one, Go find a ref-uge there— In Him who bore thy heav-y
3. The door is o-pen doubting one, Then quick-ly haste a-way; Nor tar-ry till the morrow's

Chorus.

cross Where Je-sus died for thee.) His blood can wash a-way thy sin, And
head, And knows thy ev-'ry care.)
dawn, But seek thy Lord to-day.) wash a-way, can wash a-way thy sin.

make thy spir-it free: Go lay thy bur-den at the cross, Where Je-sus died for thee.
heav-y bur-den, at the blessed cross.

Copyright, 1887, by The Ogden & Ma... Co.

ONLY WAIT A LITTLE WHILE.

IDA SCOTT TAYLOR.

FRANK M. DAVIS.

1. Christ's delays are not de-ni-als, Wait on Him a lit-tle while; Nev-er mind your cares and tri-als
2. He requires your best employment, Wait on Him a lit-tle while; He will give you pure en-joy-ment,
3. Christ's delays are not de-ni-als, Wait on Him a lit-tle while; Stand by Him and bear your trials.

On-ly wait a lit-tle while; Soon your pathway He will brighten, Soon your burden He will light-en.
On-ly wait a lit-tle while; Then go on, His name confess-ing, And the throne of grace ad-dress-ing,
On-ly wait a lit-tle while; Bide His time and trust Him, knowing He will bless the seed thou'rt sowing,

Chorus.

Soon your rap - ture He will light en, On - ly wait a lit - tle while.
He will send His promised blessing, On - ly wait a lit - tle while. } On His bless - ed word re -
In thy com - ing or thy go - ing, On - ly wait a lit - tle while.

Copyright, 1895, by The Biglow & Main Co.

ONLY WAIT A LITTLE WHILE.—Concluded.

ly, He will answer by and by, Trust a-lone in Christ your Saviour, Watch and wait a little while.

I'LL ALWAYS GO TO JESUS.

WILLARD P. MORRIS.

Arr.

1. I'll al-ways go to Je-sus, When troubled or distrest, And ev-er find a ref-uge Up-on His lov-ing breast.
2. I'll al-ways go to Je-sus, And He will come to me, In times of joy or sor-row, Whate'er my need may be.
3. I'll al-ways go to Je-sus, No mat-ter when or where, And seek His gracious presence, Find rest and ref-uge there.

A ref-uge, a ref-uge, a ref-uge, His lov-ing breast, He'll ev-er be to me, From sor-row, sin and care.

FINE.

D.S.

Copyright, 1892, by The Bigelow & Main Co.

GEMS FOR HIS CROWN.

W. A. O.

W. A. OGDEN.

1. Like gems we may shine in the crown of our King, Re-splendent with glo-ry His prais-es may tell;
2. Like lambs of the fold in His pas-ture be-low, We're fed by His grace ev-ery morning a-new;
3. Like sheep we will fol-low our Shepherd di-vine, Till life and its jour-ney on earth shall be o'er:

Redeemed by His blood, we the glad song may sing, In cho-rus e-ter-nal its numbers shall swell.
De-fend-ed, pro-tect-ed wher-ev-er we go, Led on by our Sav-iour and Shepherd so true.
Then raised in His likeness, we ev-er shall shine As stars in His crown, on the bright golden shore.

Chorus.

We shall shine in His crown, We shall shine in His crown,
We shall shine in His crown, We shall shine in His crown;

Copyright 1890, by The Bigelow & Main Co.

GEMS FOR HIS CROWN.—Concluded.

We shall shine in the man-sions a-bove.

Thro' His grace, thro' His love, thro' His grace,
thro' His love.

LIGHT BEYOND.

MARIA STRAUB.

S W STRAUB

1. Pass-ing thro' the lone-ly val-ley, Pilgrim ne'er de-spond: See, oh see the golden gleam-ing!
2. Pass-ing thro' the si-lent val-ley, Dim our mor-tal sight, Yet by faith we see the glo-ry,
3. Fear not then, tot'read the val-ley, Walk in faith's pure light. For the Lord will go be-side us,

D.S.—And at last re'll reach the mansions.

D. S.

Chorus.

FINE.

There is light (There is light) be - yond, { Light is beam-ing, } From the throne on high :
In the land (In the land) of light, { bright-ly gleam-ing }
There shall be (There shall be) no night.

In the home on high.

In the home on high.

(Copyright 1878 per S. W. Straub.)

A CROWN FOR JESUS.

Mrs. E. C. ELLSWORTH.

J. H. TENNEY.

1. Go bring the best of treas-ures, The sil - ver, and the gold; To make a crown for
2. Go search the lands of dark - ness, Where diamonds hid - den lie, And bring them to the
3. Go search the depths of o - cean, The cost - ly pearls are there; Go set them in their
4. This crown of pre - cious jew - els, Is not of earth - ly mould; A - dorned with souls im -

Chorus.

Je - sus, Let love her wealth un - fold.
Sav - iour, His crown to beau - ti - fy.
white - ness, Be - side the dia - monds fair.
mor - tal, Its wealth can ne'er be told.

A crown, a crown for Je - sus! bring ev - 'ry love - ly gem, To make for Christ the Sav - iour A roy - al di - a - dem!

Copyright, 1895, by The Biglow & Main Co.

THIS SAME JESUS.

W. A. OGDEN.

W. A. O.

1. I have heard of Je - sus in Beth - le - hem born, Of whom it hath been said, That a
2. I have heard of Je - sus on Gal - i - lee's wave; The wind o - beyed His will, And the
3. I have heard of Je - sus at Beth - a - ny's home, When standing by the grave, How He
4. I have heard of Je - sus on Cal - va - ry's brow, — He died a Sav - iour true, And He
5. I have heard of Je - sus in sep - ul - chre laid, In death's dark sul - len gloom, How He

Chorus.

star, the wise men followed from far, Till they reach'd His low - ly bed.
sea grew calm at hearing His voice. In the wondrous, "peace be still."
cried, "Come forth O Laz - a - rus now." In His might - y pow'r to save.
said, "Forgive them, Father, I pray, For they know not what they do."
burst the bars, and rising, came forth, Mighty Vic - tor from the tomb.

He is my Sav - iour!

This same Je - sus of whom I've heard, He is my Sav - iour! I've found it in His word.

Copyright, 1893, by The Biglow & Main Co.

GLORIFY HIS NAME.

W. A. COCHRAN, arr.

W. A. COCHRAN.

1. O praise the Lord, let ev-ery na - tion Glo - ri - fy His name! O praise the
2. The Sav - iour died, but now He liv - eth, Glo - ri - fy His name! His pard-'ning
3. O praise the Lord for ev - ery bless - ing, Glo - ri - fy His name! Be ev - er -

Rock of our sal - va - tion, Glo - ri - fy His name!
grace to us He giv - eth, Glo - ri - fy His name!
more His name confess - ing, Glo - ri - fy His name!

For His truth a-bid-ing ev - er, For His love no pow'r can sever,— Glo - ri - fy His name!
Thro' His all a-ton-ing mer - it, For the witness of the Spir - it, Glo - ri - fy His name!
Trusting Him, what e'er betide us, In His arms He'll safely hide us, Glo - ri - fy His name!

For His word that changeth nev-er,
For the life we may in - her - it,
Trusting Him a-lone to guide us,

FINE.

D. S. For the love He freely gave us, Glo - ri - fy His name!

Copyright, 1895, by The Bigelow & Main Co.

GLORIFY HIS NAME!- Concluded.

65
D.S.

Glo-ri-fy His name! Glo-ri-fy His name, His ho-ly name!
Glo-ri-fy His name! Glo-ri-fy His name!

SHEPHERD WITH THY TEND'REST LOVE.

WILLARD P. MORRIS.

Anon, 1865.

1. Shepherd with Thy tend'rest love Guide me to Thy fold a-bove; Let me hear Thy gen-tle voice,
2. Fill'd by Thee my cup o'erflows, For Thy love no lim - it knows; Guardian an-gel ev - er nigh,
3. Je - sus with Thy presence blest, Death is life, and life is rest; Guide me while I draw my breath,

More and more in Thee re-joice: From Thy full-ness grace receive, Ev - er in Thy Spir - it live.
Lead and draw my soul on high; Con-stant to my lat-est end, Thou my footsteps will at-tend.
Guard me thro' the gate of death; And at last, oh, let me stand, With the blest at Thy right hand.

Copyright, 1895, by The Bigelow & Main Co.

BE LOYAL TO JESUS.

IDA SCOTT TAYLOR.

W. A. OGDEN.

1. What - ev - er you do, where - ev - er you go, Be loy - al to Je - sus, your King;
2. Tho' tempt-ed and tried, stand close by His side, Be loy - al to Je - sus, your King;
3. Tho' foes may an - noy, still serve Him with joy, Be loy - al to Je - sus, your King;
4. Go spread the glad word, and sing of the Lord, Be loy - al to Je - sus, your King.

Oh serve Him a - right, and walk in the light, Be loy - al to Je - sus, your King.
Through faith in His name, the vic - to - ry claim, Be loy - al to Je - sus, your King.
Though dan - ger and doubt en - com - pass a - bout, Be loy - al to Je - sus, your King.
Your an - thems of praise tri - um-phant-ly raise, Be loy - al to Je - sus, your King.

Chorus.

Be loy - al to Je - sus, and true. Be loy - al and true.
Be loy - al and true, His arm will sus-tain thee, His strength will renew:

Be loy - - - al to Je - sus, and true. His arm and true, His arm
thy strength will re - new,

Copyright, 1883, by The Biglow & Main Co.

BE LOYAL TO JESUS.—Concluded.

Walk close to Him ev-er, His cross keep in view. Be loy-al to Je-sus, your King.

THOU THINKEST LORD, OF ME.

Rev. E. S. Lorenz.

E. D. Mund.

f.

1. A-mid the tri-als that I meet, A-mid the thorns that pierce my feet; One tho't re-mains su-
2. The cares of life come thronging fast, Up-on my soul their shadows cast; Their gloom remind-my
3. Let shadows come, let shadows go, Let life be bright, or dark with woe. I am con-tent for

D. S.—What need I fear when
D. S.

Fine. Chorus.

premely sweet, Thou thinkest Lord, of me.) Thou thinkest Lord, of me, Thou thinkest Lord of me,
heart at last, Thou thinkest Lord, of me.)
this I know, Thou thinkest Lord, of me.)

me, of me

Thou art near, And thinkest Lord, of me.

me, of me.

Copyright 1896 by E. S. Lorenz. Used by per.

KEEP STEP WITH THE MASTER.

IDA S. TAYLOR.

W. A. OGDEN.

1. Keep step with the Mas-ter, what-ev - er be-tide; Tho' dark be the pathway, keep close to your Guide,
2. Keep step with the Mas-ter, wherev - er you go; Thro' darkness and shadow, the way He will show,
3. Keep step with the Mas-ter, nor halt by the way; Whate'er He commands you, oh, haste to o - bey!

While foes are al-lur-ing, and dan-ger is near, When walk-ing with Je-sus you've nothing to fear.
The light of His presence your path will illume. And make all the des-ert a gar-den of bloom.
A - rise at His bidding, press on in His might; While walk-ing with Je-sus, you're sure to be right.

Chorus.

Keeping step . . . go brave-ly for-ward, And thy cour - . . age still re - new, . . .
keeping step,

And thy courage still re - new, still renew.

Copyright, 1894, by The Biglow & Main Co.

KEEP STEP WITH THE MASTER.—Concluded.

Dai - ly walk . with Christ your Sav-iour, He will lead you all the jour-ney through.

dai - ly walk

GO THOU IN FAITH.

W. P. M

W. P. MORRS

1. Go thou in faith to the Sav - iour,
2. Go in thy joy, to the Mas - ter,
3. He is a 'Friend ev-er pre - cious,

Tell Him thy grief and thy care, Go with thy burden of
There in His presence re-joice; Make Him thy 'Rock,' and thy
He is a 'Friend ev-er true, Wor - thy of all ad - o -

D. S.—Go thou in faith, to the

FINE.

sor - row,
'Ref - uge,
ta - tion.

Je - sus thy bur - den will bear.)
Make Him thy 'hope' and thy 'choice.' }
He is the Sav - iour for you)

Go,

Go thou in faith.

Go thou in faith.

D. S.

Go,

Sav - iour, Sure - ly He 'll an - swer thy prayer.

Copyright, 1896, by The Biglow & Main Co.

70

BE GLAD AND REJOICE.

WM. H. GARDNER.

WILLARD P. MORRIS.

1. The vales and fields with prais - es ring, And sweet the wood - land warblers sing; So
2. The sunbeams of His glo - ry tell, The flow - ers praise Him in the dell; The
3. The might - y waves in cho - rus grand, Sound out His prais - es o'er the land; The
4. While na - ture sends her praise a - long, Let us, the tune - ful strain prolong; O

Lord to Thee, Thy chil - dren raise A loud and joy - ful song of praise.
brook - let as it flows a - long, Sends up a sweet thanks - giv - ing song.
roll - ing thun - ders of the sky, Pro - claim His might - y maj - es - ty.
God, we praise Thee, and pro - claim The pow'r and glo - ry of Thy name !

Chorus. *Spirited.*

Praise Him with timbrel and harp, Praise Him with heart, and with voice, and with voice.
Praise Him with harp.

Copyright, 1895, by The Biglow & Main Co.

BE GLAD AND REJOICE.—Concluded.

His prais-es sound forth, all o - ver the earth, Let His children be glad and re - joice.
re-joice.

HAPPY DAYS. (Primary.)

CHAS. K. LANGLEY.

C. K. L.

1. Hap - py days are com - ing, go - ing, Hap - py youth-ful days; And our hearts with
2. Hap - py days are com - ing, go - ing, Joy - ous sun - ny days; While the seed of
3. Hap - py days are com - ing, go - ing, Soon our youth is past; But the seed we're

FINE. Chorus.

D.S.—Thro' them may our

D.S.

Happy days, youthful days, Happy sunny days,

joy o'er flowing, Thrill in glad-some days,
truth we're sowing, In the thorn-y ways,
dai - ly sow-ing, Grow-eth sure and fast.

lives be tell - ing Of the Saviour's praise

Copyright by Chas. K. Langley

HIS MERCY CROWNS THEM ALL.

IDA SCOTT TAYLOR.

W. A. OGDEN.

1. O ver - y, ver - y precious, God's goodness is to me! His love is full and boundless,
2. When I a - rise at morn-ing, And greet the glowing sun, Or, when the twi-light gath - ers,
3. How great the depth and rich - es Of God's e - ter - nal grace! His maj - es - ty and wis - dom

His grace di - vine and free; Each priv - i - lege and bless - ing How - ev - er great or small,
And wea - ry day is done; My heart ascends in prais - es, As on His name I call;
Ex - tend thro' time and space; He gives ten thousand blessings, But best of these we call

Chorus.

He gives from His a - bundance—His mer - cy crowns them all.
His ben - e - fits are le - gion—His mer - cy crowns them all. O won - der-ful and beau-ti-ful
The gift of Christ our Sav - iour—His mer - cy crowns them all.

Copyright, 1895, by The Bigelow & Main Co.

HIS MERCY CROWNS THEM ALL.—Concluded.

The gifts of God so free; But oh, the dearest of them all Is Christ, who died for me.

ONLY BELIEVE.

O. S. G.

Rev. O. S. Grinnell.

1. { Je-sus Christ is ev-er with us, On-ly believe. }
   { He is here to bless and save us, (Omit.) } On-ly believe. He is lov-ing, kind and gra-cious, And His blood is ef-fi-ca-cions, Ev-ery soul may find Him precious, On - ly be-lieve.

2. { Je-sus comes to sancti-fy us, On-ly believe. }
   { And His blood will pu-ri-fy us, (Omit.) } On-ly believe. Us from sin He will de-liv-er, He of life th'e-ter-nal Giv-er, Trust Him now and trust Him ever, On - ly be-lieve.

By per. of the Author.

WHAT HAST THOU DONE?

LAURA E. NEWELL.

FRANK J. ROBERTSON.

1. What hast thou done for Je - sus, O soul of mine to - day? Hast thou His er - rands
2. What hast thou done for Je - sus, Who bled and died for thee? Bear-est thou still thy
3. What hast thou done for Je - sus, To aid the weak and old? Hast thou in pit - y
4. What hast thou done for Je - sus? Is all thy life for Him? Safe - ly He'll lead thee

quick - ly run, From cross each day, And cheered the faint, And by the hand To

ear - ly morn till dost thou e'er His lis - tened to a home, and rest, and

st of sun, With voice o - bey, Who souls' complaint. To Fa - ther-land. Where

joy - ful heart al - calls.—"Come, fol-low strengthen and make skies are nev - er

way? me?" glad? dim.

Refrain.

What hast thou done? What hast thou done? What hast thou done for Je - sus to - day?

Copyright, 1892, by The Biglow & Main Co.

WHAT HAST THOU DONE?– Concluded.

rit.

What hast thou done, What hast thou done? What hast thou done for Je - sus to - day?

KEEP ME THINE. (Primary.)

FANNY J. CROSBY.

FRANK M. DAVIS.

1. Teach my lit - tle hands and feet Use - ful, Lord, to be; Tell me some-thing I can do—
2. Teach my tongue a word to speak, Gen - tle, soft and low, Make me like a beam of light;
3. Teach me how to love Thy word. Love it more and more; Help me Lord, to work for Thee,

Chorus.

Ev - ery day for Thee. } Keep me Thine, keep me Thine, Blessed Saviour keep me Thine,
Ev - ery where I go. } Keep me Thine, keep me Thine, Blessed Saviour *(omit . . .)* keep me Thine.
Till my life is o'er. }

Copyright, 1895, by The Biglow & Main Co.

76

A SONG OF RESCUE.

LAURA E. NEWELL.

W. A. OGDEN.

1. Go and seek for souls a-stray, bring them in, ... Go and res - cue them to - day
2. Go and tell them of the Lord cru - ci - fied, ... Go and tell them of the cross
3. Tho' a - far from Christ they rove, bring them in, ... Tell them of the home a - bove

bring them in

from their sin; Tell them ten - der - ly the sto - ry of the bless - ed King of glo - ry,
where He died; Tell how glad - ly He would save them From the sins that doth en-slave them,
they may win; Tho' His laws they are trans-gress-ing, Je - sus hath for each a bless-ing,

Go and help them an im-mor - tal crown to win.
And that, for His own to have them, Je - sus died.
If they come their sins con-fess - ing un - to Him.

Chorus.

Bring them in, bring them in from the
Let them come, come to - day, from the

Copyright, 1896, by The Biglow & Main Co.

A SONG OF RESCUE.—Concluded.

tempting paths of sin, Bring them in . . . Bring them in;

paths of sin a way;Come to - day . . Omit . . . .) Come to - day. . . .

bring them in;

come to-day . . . .

to - day. . . .

CHILDREN'S PRAISE.

W. P. M.

JOHN HENLEY.

1. Children of Je - ru - sa - lem, Sang the praise of Je - sus'name;Children, too, of lat - er days.
2. We are taught to love the Lord, We are taught to read His word, We are taught the way to heav'n,
3. Par-ents, teachers, old and young,All u - nite to swell the song; Higher and yet high-er rise,

p Refrain.

Join to sing the Saviour's praise.)
Praise to God for all he giv'n. } Hark!hark!hark! while infant voices sing Loud hosannas to our King.
Till ho-san-nas reach the skies.)

Copyright, 1895, by The Biglow & Main Co.

78

FRUITS OF THE SPIRIT.

W. L. BENNETT.

CHAS. EDW. POLLOCK.

1. There's a love that's be-got-ten with-in When the work of re-demp-tion is done;
2. There's a joy of unspeak-a-ble worth, 'Tis more pre-cious than tongue can de-fine;
3. There's a place like a riv-er, that flows Pure and sweet from the bright realms of day—
4. May our hearts with this love o-ver-flow, Un-to us may this rap-ture be given;

When the soul is de-liv-ered from sin Thro' the blood of the cru-ci-fied One.
Je-sus brought the rich gift to the earth From His king-dom of glo-ry di-vine.
That our bless-ed Redeem-er be-stows Up-on all who His pre-cepts o-bey.
May this peace be our por-tion be-low, Our re-ward in the king-dom of heav'n.

Chorus.

By and by, By and by, By and by, by and by, We shall dwell in the full-ness of love,

Copyright, 1885, by The Biglow & Main Co.

FRUITS OF THE SPIRIT.—Concluded.

In the blest . . . home on high, . . In the beau-ti-ful man-sions a-bove.
In the blest, in the blest home on high,

PRAISE YE THE FATHER.

F. F. FLEMMING

1. Praise ye the Fa-ther for His lov-ing kind-ness, Ten-der-ly cares He for His lov-ing
2. Praise ye the Sav-iour, great is His com-pas-sion, Gra-cious-ly cares He for His cho-sen
3. Praise ye the Spir-it, Comfort-er of Is-rael, Sent of the Fa-ther and the Son to

chil-dren; Praise Him, ye an-gels, praise Him in the heav-ens, Praise ye Je-ho-vah!
peo-ple; Young men and maid-ens, ye old men and chil-dren, Praise ye the Sav-iour!
bless us; Praise ye the Fa-ther, Son, and Ho-ly Spir-it, Praise the Tri-unne God!

OVERCOMING IN HIS NAME.

Miss J. WILSON.

W. A. OGDEN.

1. In the ho - ly Christian war-fare, We the help of Christ may claim; And thro' grace di-vine may
2. Tho' the foes we meet be ma - ny, Sure - ly we have naught to fear, Trusting in the "Friend of
3. Let us nev - er be disheartened, Or in weakness yield to strife; But be loy - al to our
4. To each soul that o - ver-com-eth, Fade-less palms in heaven be-long; Where beyond all sound of

Refrain.

con - quer, O - ver - coming thro' His name. O - ver-coming thro' His name, . . O-ver
sin - ners, Who is ev - er, ev - er near.
Lead - er, And ob - tain the crown of life.
con - flict, Swells the vic-tor's glad new song.

His name,

coming thro' His name: Praise the Lord! we shall be vic-tors, O-ver-coming thro' His name.

Copyright, 1894, by The Biglow & Main Co.

O GUIDING STAR.

W. P. M.

WILLARD P. MORRIS.

1. The star that shone o'er Beth-le-hem, Is shin-ing now for me, To guide my feet thro'
2. Its rays are streaming from a-bove, Thro' God's own word so true, They fill my soul with
3. O may I like the men of old, Be-hol. O Star, by Thee, Un - til I reach my

tan - gled paths, Dear Sav - iour, un - to Thee.)
sweet - er peace, Than sin - ners ev - er knew. }
heav - only home, And my De - liv - er - er see.)

Chorus.

O bless - ed Star, O ra-diant Light: shine

on me from a - far, And guide me to my home a-bove, Where ma-ny mansions are.

Copyright, 1893, by The Biglow & Main Co.

82

WHAT A MEETING THAT WILL BE!

W. A. O.

W. A. OGDEN.

1. When we gath-er by and by, In our bless-ed home on high, What a meet-ing, what a
2. When we gath-er on that shore, There to dwell for-ev-er-more, What a meet-ing, what a
3. When the an-gel reap-ers come, With the last sheaf gathered home, What a meet-ing, what a

meet-ing that will be! . . . . We shall know each oth-er there. Where the ho-ly an-gels are;
meet-ing that will be! . . . . There our Sav-iour we shall greet, Cast our crowns be-fore His feet;
meet-ing that will be! . . . . For, by grace di-vine we'll stand, Robed and crowned at God's right hand;

D.S.—Hal-le-lu-jah's sweet, That the ran-somed there re-peat,

that will be!

FINE. Chorus.

What a meet-ing, what a meet-ing that will be! What a meet-ing that will be, Yon-der

To the Lamb up-on the throne, for-ev-er-more.

Copyright, 1895, by The Biglow & Main Co.

WHAT A MEETING THAT WILL BE!—Concluded.

by the crys-tal sea. When we gath-er with our friends gone be - fore; Mid the
gone be - fore;

CAMPING IN THE WILDERNESS.

EDEN R. LATTA.   D. W. CRIST.

1. { Camp-ing in the wil-der-ness, Jour-ney-ing to Ca-naan; } Jour-ney-ing to Ca-naan.
   { Here we've no a - bid-ing place, (Omit. . . . to Ca-naan;)
2. { Camp-ing in the wil-der-ness, Jour-ney-ing to Ca-naan; } Jour-ney-ing to Ca-naan.
   { Like old Is - ra - el, we press, (Omit. . . . to Ca-naan;)
3. { Camp-ing in the wil-der-ness, Jour-ney-ing to Ca-naan; } Jour-ney-ing to Ca-naan.
   { Spite of toil and wea-ri-ness, (Omit. . . .)

Chorus.

{ Soon we'll cross the riv - er, Soon we'll dwell a-mong the blest, } In the heaven-ly Ca-naan rest.
{ Soon we'll cross the riv - er, (Omit. . . .)

Copyright, 1890, by D. W. Crist. Used by per.

LITTLE SOLDIERS OF THE KING.

LAURA E. NEWELL.

C. K. LANGLEY.

May be used as Marching song.

1. We are lit-tle sol-diers. Sol-diers of the Lord, Trusting in the Saviour, Leaning on His word.
2. Christ our mighty Cap-tain, Guards us on the way, As we march tow'rd heaven, Un - to Him we pray.
3. Keep us pure, dear Saviour, Valiant, brave and strong; Help us to be faith-ful, And avoid the wrong:

He sus-tains and keeps us, In the ways of truth, We have come to Je-sus, Him we give our youth.
Pa-tient-ly He list - ens, To our feeb-lest pray'r, For He takes the children, In His tend-er care.
Keep us ev - er near Thee, Clo-ser to Thy side; May we live for ev - er, True to Him who died.

Chorus.

We are lit-tle sol-diers, Sol-diers of the King, Marching 'neath His banner, Loyal hearts we bring.

Copyright, 1893, by The Bigelow & Main Co.

THE SHEPHERD'S CRY.

W. A. O.
GEO. C. HUGG

Duet.

1. Like sheep in the des-ert we're stray-ing, O'er mount-ains wild and bare,
2. In tones that are gen-tle and plead-ing, We hear Him kind-ly say,
3. Oh heed the sweet voice of the Shep-herd, "Re-turn ye to the fold,

"Come
say,
"Come

Chorus. *Spirited.*

way from the fold of the Shep-herd, And from His ten-der care.
hith-er my sheep that have wan-dered, From me so far a-way."
dwell with my flock safe-ly guard-ed From dan-ger, storm, and cold."

Re-turn, re-turn, re-

turn! O hear the Shepherd's cry: Re-turn, re-turn, re-turn! For why will ye die.

Copyright, 1896, by The Biglow & Main Co.

CHILDREN MAY BE HERALDS.

JULIA STERLING.

CHAS. H. GABRIEL.

1. Lit - tle chil-dren may be her-alds of the great sal - va-tion, They may tell of our Re-
2. Lit - tle chil-dren have their mission in the Mas - ter's ser - vice, They can smile a - way the
3. Lit - tle chil-dren are re-mem-bered in the Sav - iour's promise, They may car - ly share the

deem-er and the cross He bore; By their grate-ful Sab-bath off'rings they can send the Bi - ble
sor-rows and the clouds of care: O'er the worn and wea - ry spir - it, that with grief is pin - ing.
blessings of re-deem-ing grace; He is watch-ing kind-ly o'er them, and His word as - sures us

That will cheer the hearts of ma - ny on a far - off shore.
They can drop a word of kind-ness like a sun-beam fair.
That in heav'n their an-gels ev - er see the Fa - ther's face.

Chorus.

Lit - tle chil - dren

Lit - tle chil-dren may be her-alds,

Copyright, 1895, by The Biglow & Main Co.

CHILDREN MAY BE HERALDS.—Concluded.

may be her-alds, joy-ful her-alds of the blessed Sav-iour's love, Lit - tle children

blessed her-alds of sal - va-tion.

chil - dren may be her-alds, gladly point-ing ma-ny to the home a - bove.

may be her-alds, blessed her-alds of sal-va-tion,

Lit-tle children

A CHEERFUL GIVER.

W. A. O.

W. A. OGDEN.

Choir. *After collection.*

School.

1

2

1. The Lord loveth a cheerful giv - er, { Therefore with gladness we will bring }
   { Now un-to Christ, our (*Omit.*) } of - fer-ing.

2. The Lord love a cheerful giv - er, { Therefore with joy we now proclaim }
   { Prais-es un-to His (*Omit.*) } ho-ly name. A - men.

Copyright, 1895, by The Biglow & Main Co.

DOWN ALONG THE AGES.

FANNIE M. PARKER.

R. A. GLENN.

1. Down a - long the roll-ing a - ges, Rings a prom-ise ev - er sweet, Bring-ing com-fort, joy; and
2. Tho' we oft may tread the pathway All be - set with danger wild, Still the promise of the
3. What - so - ev - er be our mis - sion, Wheth-er hum-ble, great or small, Je - sus lov-ing - ly hath
4. Let us nev-er doubt nor fal - ter Let us nev-er wea-ry grow, Knowing well the bless-ed

Chorus.

glad - ness, For the wea - ry faltering feet.
Mas - ter Will up-hold His weakest child.
prom - ised To be with us thro' it all.
Sav - iour Lead-eth still wher-e'er we go.

Bless - ed prom - ise full of com - fort,

From our best and tru - est Friend, "Fear ye not, for I am with you," Ev - er with you

Copyright, 1890, by The Biglow & Main Co.

DOWN ALONG THE AGES.—Concluded.

to the end; "Fear ye not for I am with you," Ev - er with you to the end.

MY REST IS OVER YONDER.

I. D. K.

W. A. OGDEN

1. In a wea-ry land I wan-der, 'Mid the tempest's fearful shock. But my home is o - ver yon-der,
2. Here my toils are un - a - bat-ing, but I know they'll soon be o'er, By the Rock of my Sal - va - tion,
3. In those pastures fair and ver-nal, With my Shepherd's chosen flock, I will feast in joys e - ter - nal,
4. So with pa-tient faith I wan-der. Fearing not the tempest's shock. For my rest is o - ver yon-der,

D.S.—Rock of A - ges cleft for me.

FINE. Refrain.

In the shad-ow of the Rock,
I will rest me ev - er more.
In the shad-ow of the Rock.
In the shad-ow of the Rock.

Rock of A - ges cleft for me, Let me hide my-self in Thee;

Let me hide my - self in Thee.

Copyright, 1895, by The Biglow & Main Co.

WHEN THE KING DRAWS NIGH.

Wm. H. Gardner.

W. A. Ogden.

1. There's a day of judgment com-ing, And to meet it we should try, So we all must
2. If your heart is weak and sin - ful, To de - ny it do not try, For each soul is
3. If you long for joy for - ev - er, And a dwell-ing-place on high, Then be read - y

then be read - y
weighed in judg-ment
O my broth - er,

Chorus.

When the King . . . . draws nigh.
When the King . . . . draws nigh.
When the King . . . . draws nigh.
Shall we all be read-y when the

When the King

King draws nigh, When the King . . . . draws nigh. . . . Will our lamps be burn-ing bright,

When the King draws nigh, draws nigh.

Copyright, 1895, by The Biglow & Main Co.

WHEN THE KING DRAWS NIGH.—Concluded.

When He bursts up on our sight? Shall we all be read-y When the King . . . . draws nigh?

When the King

TURN TO THE LORD.

Geo. C. Hugg.

W. A. O.

1. O wea-ry pil-grim, gone a - stray, Far from the Father's house a-way; Turn to the Lord while yet you may.
2. How like the prod-i - gal of old, Many have wander'd from the fold, Out in the bitter night, and cold.
3. Now to the Father's house re-turn, Nev-er a - gain His mercy spurn! Quick-ly a-way from idols turn.

D.S.—For in His kingdom there's a place,

FINE. Chorus.

Turn to the Lord, and seek His face; Turn to the Lord, and trust His grace,

Ere fall the shades of night.
On bar-ren wilds they stray.
And seek the Lord to - day.

For ev-'ry weary soul.

D.S.

THE PARADISE OF GOD.

Rev. E. A. HOFFMAN.
DUET.

Rev. E. S. LORENZ.

There's a home, a bless - ed home, In that fair land a - bove, Where peace and hap - pi -
There's a home, a heaven-ly home, In fade - less ver-dure dressed, Where toil and la - bor
There's a home, a bless - ed home, Where care and sor - row cease, Where sin and sick - ness
In this home, this peace-ful home, Are all the saints of God, Who washed their robes, and

Chorus.

ness abound,—The Par - a - dise of Love.
are no more,—The Par - a - dise of Rest.
nev - er come,—The Par - a - dise of Peace.
made them white—In Je - sus' pre - cious blood.

This bless - ed home our gra-cious Lord, Has

purchased with His blood, That we might en - ter through the gates The Par - a - dise of God.

Copyright, 1890, by The Bigelow & Main Co.

WALKING WITH THE SAVIOUR.

Rev. M. L. HOFFORD, arr.

W. A. OGDEN.

1. Are you walk-ing with the Sav-iour   In the true and liv-ing way? Is   the meek and low-ly
2. Are you walk-ing with the Sav-iour   And re-joic-ing in His light? Is   your lamp all trimmed and
3. Are you walk-ing with the Sav-iour   Does your heart within you burn, While the sto - ry   of re -

D.S.—walk-ing with the Sav-iour   In the true and liv-ing way?   Is   the meek and low-ly

FINE.

Je - sus Your compan-ion ev-ery   day?   Are you whol-ly con-se-crat-ed   To the ser-vice
burn-ing Is   it shin-ing clear and bright? Are the poor   in cot-tage low - ly,   And the stran-ger
demption From the word of life you learn? And when soft - ly   fall the shad-ows   At the tran-quil

Je - sus Your com-pan-ion   ev - ery day?

D.S.

of   the Lord? Do you find sweet rest and com-fort   In   the teach-ing   of   His word?
by   the way   Ev - er   blest   by words of kind-ness   Which in love they hear you   say? Are you
eve-ning tide.   Do   you pray Him still to   tar - ry,   And with-in your home   a - bide?)

Arrangement of words Copyright, 1895, by The Bigelow Main Co.

94

I WILL TRUST THEE.

FANNY J. CROSBY.

WILLARD P. MORRIS.

1. I am cling-ing, O my Sav-iour, To the prom-ise Thou hast made;
2. I am rest-ing, O my Sav-iour, At the cross where Thou hast died;
3. I am look-ing, O my Sav-iour, For Thy smile of love di - vine;
4. I am wait-ing, O my Sav-iour, I am long-ing for the day

That Thy grace will keep me
I am rest-ing, and be -
In the brightness of its
When these doubts will all be

Chorus.

I will trust Thee, I will trust Thee, I will trust Thee, O my Sav-iour, Till my faith is lost in sight.

ev - er, If my trust on Thee is staid.
liev - ing, In my soul Thou wilt a - bide.
glo - ry, Thro' the rift - ing clouds to shine.
o - ver, And the mists be rolled a - way.

I will trust Thee, In the darkness, or the light;

Copyright, 1895, by The Biglow & Main Co.

BEAR THE KINGS MESSAGE.

Wm H. GARDNER.

W. A. OGDEN.

1. The King has need of sol-diers His vic-to-ries to win, And some must bear His mes-sage
2. The King will give His ar-mor A breast-plate, sword and shield; His name is on the ban-ner
3. The King will lead us on-ward A-gainst the hosts of sin; Why do you lin-ger long-er?
4. Oh, bear the gos-pel mes-sage, Tho' per-ils block your way; For God will send His an-gels

Chorus.

To souls now lost in sin.
You bear up-on the field.
To-day the fight be-gin.
To guard you day by day.

Bear the Kings message o'er land and sea. Je-sus is call-ing for

you and me; Hast-en with gladness, oh, hear His call. Bear the Kings message to one and all.

Copyright, 1897, by The Biglow & Main Co.

RICH IN GRACE.

96 W. B. WILLIAMS.

FRANK J. ROBERTSON.

1. Rich in grace, O Sav-iour make me, Grace to help in time of need; Rich in patience when af-
2. Rich in faith in Thee, my Sav-iour, Faith to drive all doubts a-way, Rich in love to my Cre-
3. Rich in joy, O Saviour make me, Scatt'ring sunshine all a-round, Rich in pur-i-ty of

flict-ed, Rich in many a no-ble deed. Rich in life of con-se-cra-tion, To the
a-tor. And to man, tho' gone a-stray. Rich in hope of reach-ing heav-en, Tho' cast
pur-pose, Rich in love, may I be found. Rich in com-fort-ing the mourn-er, In for-

FINE.

f.

ser-vice of the Lord. Rich in growth, and ripe fru-i-tion Rich in knowledge of the word.
down, in deep de-spair, Rich to know of sins for-giv-en, Rich in faith and hum-ble prayer.
give-ness of a sin, Rich in time, and rich for-ev-er. For God's kingdom is with-in.

D.S.—Ev-er trust-ing in the prom-ise, Till I see my Saviour's face.

Copyright, 1897, by The Biglow & Main Co.

RICH IN GRACE.— Concluded.

97

Chorus.

Rich in grace. Rich in grace, ev - er rich in grace,
rich in grace, rich in grace, I would run the Chris-tian race.

PRAY FOR REAPERS.

WILLARD P. MORRIS.

A. L. V.

1. Saints of God the day is bright'ning, Token of our com-ing Lord, O'er the earth the fields are whit'ning
2. Free-bly now they toil in sad-ness, Weeping o'er the waste around, Slowly gath'ring grains of gladness
3. Now, O Lord, ful-fill Thy pleasure, Breathe upon Thy chosen band, And with pen - ti - tcos - tal measure

Loud-er rings the Master's word, Pray for reapers, pray for reap - ers In the vine-yard of the Lord.
While their earnest cries resound, Pray for reapers, pray for reap - ers That the work may yet a-bound.
Faithful reapers, faith-ful reap - ers, Send Thy reap-ers o'er the land.

Copyright 1895, by The Bigelow & Main Co.

COME TO THE FOUNTAIN.

W. P. M.

W. A. OGDEN.

1. The fount-ain of life is flow-ing, Is flow-ing for all to - day; Then hast-en to
2. The fount-ain of life is flow-ing, Is flow-ing for all to - day; Then hast-en to
3. The fount-ain of life is flow-ing, Is flow-ing for all to - day; Then hast-en to

DUET.

drink of its wa - ters! Oh quick-ly the call o - bey. Come to the fount-ain, the
drink of its wa - ters! Oh quick-ly the call o - bey. Come with-out mon - ey, oh,
drink of its wa - ters! Oh quick-ly the call o - bey. Heark-en the Bride and the

wa - ter free, Flow-eth for all who may thirs-ty be; Je - sus in mer - cy is call - ing thee.
now draw near, Lin - ger no long-er in doubt and fear, Je - sus will give you this wa - ter clear.
Spir - it say: "Come whoso - ev - er will, to - day," Here at the fount-ain thy thirst al - lay,

Copyright, 1895, by The Biglow & Main Co.

COME TO THE FOUNTAIN.—Concluded.

Full Chorus.

Chorus.

To drink of the fountain of life.
That flows from the fountain of life.
Come drink of the wa-ter of life.

Oh, come to the foun - ain! Come to the

Come to the fount, come to the fount, opened for sin.

fount - - ain! Come to the foun' - ain. and drink of the wa-ter of life.

opened for sin, Come to the fount. (Come to the fount, and

HE GUARDETH THEE AND ME.

Arr.

W. P. M...RRIS.

1. He who gave the sunlight, Pale and silver moonlight, And the glist'ning sun-light, Guardeth thee and me.
2. He who guides the river, Glid-ing onward ev - er, Nev - er asking whith-er, Guardeth thee and me.
3. He who made the flowers, Hills and woods and bowers, Tempests, clouds and showers, Guardeth thee and me.

Copyright, 1896, by The Biglow & Main Co.

WORKING AND WAITING.

H. G. JACKSON D. D.

Mrs. W. S. NICKLE.

1. Work-ing for the Mas-ter in the har - vest field, Paus-ing not for wea - ri-ness or pain,
2. Work-ing in the vineyard, toil-ing for the Lord, Faith-ful-ly from dawn to set of sun;
3. Wait-ing for the Mas-ter in the Beu-lah land, Wait-ing till the welcome summons come;

Joy - ful in His ser - vice, I the sick - le wield, Gath'ring precious sheaves of gold-en grain,
Sweet will be the rest-ing, rich be my re-ward, When to me the Lord shall say, "well done,"
Bid - ding me cross o - ver to the gold - en strand, There to dwell with Him in bliss at home.

Chorus.

Work - ing . . . work - ing . . . Work - ing till the time of rest shall come; . . .

Work-ing, work-ing for the Mas-ter,

rit.

shall come;

Copyright, by W. S. Nickle. Used by per.

WORKING AND WAITING. —Concluded.

ril......

THOS. MACKELLAR.

Wait - ing, ... Wait - ing for His plea - sure,
Wait - ing, wait - ing
wait - ing, ... Wait - ing till the Lord shall call me home.

SHEPHERD OF THE FLOCK.

J. C. WOLFE.

1. Tell me, whom my soul doth love, Where Thy flock are feed - ing; Where the pas - tures
2. Tell me, shel - tered from the heat, Where at noon they rest them; Where at night their
3. Strong is Thy pro - tect - ing arm, Rich - ly Thou pro - vid - est, Feed - ing, rest - ing

which they rove, Thou their footsteps lead - ing; Tell me, tell me, Shepherd of the flock.
safe re - treat Fold where none molest them? Tell me, tell me, Shep - herd of the flock.
kept from harm, Blest the flock Thou guid - est, Je - sus, Sav - iour, Shep - herd of the flock.

Copyright .....

HE SEEKETH THE LOST.

MISS J. WILSON.

W. A. OGDEN.

1. There is a fold of safe-ty, For all the souls that roam In sin's un-friendly des-ert,
2. With love beyond all tell-ing, The ho-ly Son of God Bore pain, reproach, and sor-row,
3. We know this faithful Shepherd, We love His gen-tle voice; And safe with-in His keep-ing,

A far from rest and home; And Christ, the Shepherd true and kind, In pit-y seeks the lost to find.
And earth's dark pathway trod To find the lost in error's night, And lead them into truth and right.
Our ransomed souls re-joice. Oh help us Lord, lost souls to win, And bring them back from paths of sin.

Chorus.

He seek - - - eth the lost . . . With ten-der-ness un - told. The lost in sin's sad
He seeketh the lost, He seeketh the lost,

Copyright, 1890, by The Biglow & Main Co.

HE SEEKETH THE LOST.—Concluded.

103

wild-er-ness, He seek-eth pa-tient-ly to bless, And lead them, and lead them In - to the fold.
Lead them into the fold.

SALUTATION, AND BENEDICTION.

WM. B. BRADBURY.

Scrip.—"Let the people praise thee, O God; let all the people praise thee."

CHORISTER.

School.

1. "O give thanks unto the Lord; for he is *good*; For his mer - cy en - dur - eth for - ev - er."
2. "O come, let us sing unto the Lord; For his mer - cy en - dur - eth for - ev - er."
3. O may He grant us His Spirit and *blessing*, "For his mer - cy en - dur - eth for - ev - er."

CHORISTER.

School.

"O give thanks unto the God of *gods*; For his mer - cy en-dur-eth for - ev - er.
Rejoice in the Lord and give Him *thanks*, "For his mer - cy en-dur-eth for - ev - er."
We will praise the Lord with our whole *heart*; "For his mer - cy en-dur-eth for - ev - er."

A - men.

ALL. "Let the words of my mouth, and the meditation of my heart, be acceptable in thy sight, O LORD, my strength, and my re-deemer."

Cor by per.

ARE YOU DRIFTING?

L. E. JONES.

L. E. JONES.

1. Looking out on life's wide ocean, Many a bark is seen to-day, Some there are with fav'ring breezes,
2. Looking out on life's wide ocean, Where the tempest rages wild, Oh, how ma - ny souls are drifting
3. Looking out on life's wide ocean, See the billows and the shoals, See the tem-pest in its fu - ry

Sailing on their homeward way, Some are on - ly drift-ing, drift-ing, Swept by ev - ery wind and tide;
By the tempter's pow'r beguiled! They are drift-ing, sure-ly drift-ing, To a dark and dis - mal shore,
As a - far and near it rolls! There are ma - ny drift-ing, drift-ing, Where the seas are roll - ing high;

Chorus.

They may nev - er make the har-bor, Nev - er reach the oth - er side,)
Where the night of sin has set-tled, And the life boat comes no more, } Brother is your vessel drift-ing,
Rouse ye lost, and seek the har-bor! Hear the Gospel's warning cry.)

Copyright, 1896, by The Biglow & Main Co.

ARE YOU DRIFTING.—Concluded.

Tempest toss'd and far a - way? While the har-bor lights are burning, Turn, O turn without de - lay.

MY REDEEMER LIVES.

SAMUEL MEDLEY.

W. P. MORRS.

1. I know that my Re-deem - er lives! What joy the blest assurance gives! He lives, He lives who
2. He lives to bless me with His love, He lives to plead for me a - bove, He lives, my hun-gry
3. He lives to grant me rich sup-ply, He lives to guide me with His eye, He lives, to com-fort

D.S. He lives my ev - er - e -

FINE. Chorus.

D.S.

He lives, He lives, O praise ye His name!

He lives. He lives.

once was dead, He lives, my ev - er-last-ing Head.
soul to feed, He lives to bless in time of need.
me when faint, He lives to hear my soul's complaint.

last - ing Friend, He lives to love me to the end.

Copyright 1895, by The Bigelow & Main Co.

BRING THEM IN. (Primary.)

ALEXCENAH THOMAS.

W. A. OGDEN.

1. Hark! 'tis the Shepherd's voice I hear, Out in the des-ert dark and drear, Call - ing the lambs that
2. Who'll go and help this Shepherd kind, Help Him the lit-tle lambs to find? Who'll bring the lost ones
3. Out in the desert, hear their cry, Out on the mountain wild and high, Hark! 'tis the Shepherd

Chorus.

roam to - day Far from the Shepherd's fold a-way.
to the fold. Where they'll be sheltered from the cold?   Bring them in, Bring them in, Bring them
speaks to thee "Go, find my lambs wher-e'er they be."

in from the fields of sin;   Bring them in, Bring them in, Bring the lit-tle ones to Je - sus.

Used by per. W. A. Ogden, owner of Copyright

SECRET PRAYER.

FANNY J. CROSBY.   W. H. DOANE

1. There is an hour of calm re-lief From ev-ery throbbing care, 'Tis when, be-fore a
2. When one by one, like threads of gold, The hues of twi-light fall, What sweet com-mun-ion
3. I hear se-raph-ic tones that float A-mid re-les-tial air. And bathe my soul in
4. O when the hour of death shall come, How sweet from thence to rise. With prayer on earth my

throne of grace, I kneel in secret prayer.
with my God, My Sav-iour and my all.
streams of joy. A-lone in secret prayer.
lat-est breath. My watchword to the skies.

Refrain.

O that voice . . tome so dear. Breathing

O that voice I love to hear, love to hear,

soft - ly on my ear! Weary child, . . look up and see; 'Tis thy Saviour speaks to thee.

Breathing softly on my ear, on my ear! Weary child, look up and see, look and see;

Copyright, 1873, by The Biglow & Main Co.

108

Dr. G. L. MITCHELL.

WATCH YE, THEREFORE.

W. A. OGDEN.

1. Watch, earnest-ly watch. The Lord's ap-proach is near-ing. Like as a thief at night is His ap-pear-ing; He com-eth to judge the
2. Work, joy-ful-ly work. All ye who know His chast-'ning; Lift up your heads, the day of rest is last'ning. Rest, glo-ri-ous rest with
3. Trust, joy-al-ly trust, And as to Him thou'rt cling-ing, Then in thy heart the blest as-sur-ance ring-ing, Know surely thy name is

man can know the hour, Like as a thief at night is His ap-pear-ing;
your re-ward is nigh, Lift up your heads, the day of rest is last'ning.
Sav-iour's blest commands, Then in thy heart the blest as-sur-ance ring-ing.

Chorus.

world in truth and pow'r. }
Je-sus by and by, } Watch ye, pray ye, soldiers of the Lord; Work ye, wait ye, trusting in His word;
writ-ten in His hands. }

Copyright, 1896, by The Biglow & Main Co.

WATCH YE, THEREFORE.—Concluded.

Keep His commandments, and His law o-bey, And He will re-ward you in the last great day.

REST, AND GROW STRONG.

M. GEORGIA ORMUND.

WILLARD P. MORRIS.

1. Dark tho' the shadows be, Stronger the light, Back of the hanging clouds, Dazzling and bright.
2. Al - ways the darkest edge, Fades in - to light, Bright, happy, sun - ny days Creep from the night.
3. God with a lov-ing hand Gives what is best; Trust in His watchful care, Trust Him and rest.

Then when the gloom is laid,—Sor-row, or wrong, Un - der the cool-ing shade Rest, and grow strong.
Flow-rets would droop and die,—Life's joys would fade, We're not the sun's hot glare, Tempered with shade.
All that He send-eth thee,—Shadow or sun, Know then, O wea-ry child, For good 'twas done.

Copyright, 1895, by The Biglow & Main Co.

HAPPY IN THEE.

110

SARAH E. JAMES.

WM. J. KIRKPATRICK.

1. My soul is re - joic-ing, and sweet is my song, While on-ward to Zi - on I jour-ney a - long;
2. Thy pres-ence is with me, Thy im - age I bear; Thy ban-ner is o'er me, Thy rai-ment I wear;
3. I walk in Thy sun-shine, I rest in Thy smile, And vis-ions of glo-ry the mo-ments be-guile;
4. I know there's a man-sion pre-par-ing a - bove, Where soon Thou wilt call me to feast on Thy love;

No thorns in my path-way, no clouds can I see, For oh, I am hap-py, dear Sav-iour, in Thee.
The world and its pleasures are noth-ing to me, For oh, I am hap-py, dear Sav-iour, in Thee.
Thy peace like a riv - er is flow-ing for me, And oh, I am hap-py, dear Sav-iour, in Thee.
Yet here while I tar-ry con-tent will I be, For oh, I am hap-py, dear Sav-iour, in Thee.

Chorus.

Hap - - py in Thee, ... hap - - py in Thee,

Hap-py in Thee, hap-py in Thee, Sav-iour, dear Sav-iour, I'm hap-py in Thee.

Copyright, 188- by Wm. J. Kirkpatrick. Used by per.

HAPPY IN THEE.— Concluded.

My soul is re-joic-ing, my spir-it is free, And oh, I am hap-py, dear Sav-iour, in Thee.

DO YOU HEAR THE SABBATH BELLS?

Arr.
M E O.

1. Lit-tle the chil-dren, listen, list-en; Do you hear the sabbath bells? Do you know the precious sto-ry
2. All the air is hush'd and ho-ly, On-ly chime the sabbath bells? List-en to the wondrous sto-ry.
3. They are tell-ing, ev - er tell-ing, Of the love of God's dear Son; How He left His Father's dwelling,
4. Now, while sabbath bells are pealing, We would send our silent prayer, From the place where saints are kneeling,

FINE.
D. S.— We would serve The blessed Je-sus,

Chorus.

That their pleas-ant chim-ing tells?
That their pleas-ant chim-ing tells?
And to sin-ful earth came down,
To our Fa-ther o - ver there.

We are lit - tle chil-dren longing To be taught the way to Thee:

D. S.

And from all that's wrong would flee.

Copyright 189_, by The Biglow & Main Co.

112

TELL IT TO JESUS.

J. E. RANKIN, D. D.

E. S. LORENZ.

1. Are you wea-ry, are you heav-y-heart-ed? Tell it to Je-sus, Tell it to Je-sus;
2. Do the tears flow down your cheeks unbid-den? Tell it to Je-sus, Tell it to Je-sus;
3. Do you fear the gath'ring clouds of sor-row? Tell it to Je-sus, Tell it to Je-sus;
4. Are you trou-bled at the thought of dy-ing? Tell it to Je-sus, Tell it to Je-sus:

FINE.

Are you griev-ing o - ver joys de-part - ed? Tell it to Je - sus a - lone.
Have you sins that to man's eye are hid - den? Tell it to Je - sus a - lone.
Are you anx - ious what shall be to-mor-row? Tell it to Je - sus a - lone.
For Christ's com-ing King-dom are you sigh - ing? Tell it to Je - sus a - lone.

D.S.—You have no oth-er such a friend or broth-er, Tell it to Je - sus a - lone.

D. S.

Chorus.

Tell it to Je - sus, Tell it to Je - sus, He is a Friend that's well known;

Copyright, 1880, by E. S. Lorenz. Used by per.

I HAVE CALLED THEE BY THY NAME.

FANNY J. CROSBY.

W. A. OGDEN.

1. Thro' the cleansing blood of Je-sus, I have found a per-fect cure, On the might-y Rock of
2. Thro' the cleansing blood of Je-sus, Constant peace in God I know; Tho' my sins were once like
3. O the joy my heart o'er flow-ing! O the song I now can sing! Glo-ry, glo-ry hal-le-

A - ges Now by faith my trust is sure. }
crim-son. He has washed them white as snow. } Bless-ed words of life and com-fort. From the
In - jah To the Lord my Sav-iour King. }

Chorus.

lips of truth that came. "Fear thou not, I have re-deemed thee. I have called thee by thy name."

Copyright, 1887, by the Biglow & Main Co.

114

SEEK HIM TO-DAY.

LAURA E. NEWELL.

W. A. OGDEN.

1. Seek Him to-day! seek Him to-day! Come to the Sav-iour, no long-er de-lay;
2. Seek Him to-day! bright is the sky; Tri-als and sor-rows will come by and by;
3. Seek Him to-day! seek Him to-day! Grieve not the Spir-it, His plead-ing o-bey;

Now in life's morning, give Je-sus your heart; He from His chil-dren will nev-er de-part.
But if you trust Him, His arm will up-hold; Haste while He's call-ing, and en-ter the fold
Je-sus is pit-i-ful, lov-ing and kind; They who will seek Him right ear-ly, shall find.

Chorus.

Come, come, Come while you may; Come, come, Seek Him to-day; Come to the

Copyright 1895, by The Biglow & Main Co

SEEK HIM TO-DAY.—Concluded.

Sav-iour, no long-er de - lay;   Seek Him to - day,   oh, seek Him to - day!

LEAD ME ON.

JAS. L. CARR.

1. Hope is steadfast, but the day. Ev - er fades in night a - way; And tho' dark appears the dawning,
2. Let me place my hand in thine; Help me by Thy pow'r di-vine; Shine, hope's beacon light, more brightly,
3. Lead me on.   O blessed Lord; Guard me with the Spirit's sword, Hear, O hear me blessed Sav-iour,

D.S.—Lead me on, oh, Master lead me,

D.S.

FINE. Refrain.

Yet, O Mas-ter, lead me on)
All my jour-ney lead me through. } Lead me on,   Lead me   on.   Let me nev-er from Thee stray,
I will fol - low Thee to - day.)

Lead me on, O   lead me on,

Then I shall not loose my way.

Copyright, 1891, by The Biglow & Main Co.

TRUSTING THEE.

FANNY J. CROSBY.

CHAS. H. GABRIEL.

116

1. Trusting Thee, O gracious Lord. Leaning on Thy faithful word. What a calm de-light is mine,
2. Trust-ing where-so-ever I go. Trusting while in tears I sow; Though of toil no fruit I see,
3. Trust-ing, tho' my friends should fail; Trusting, tho' my foes pre-vail; Trusting in the darkest hour,
4. Trust-ing Thee what e'er be-tide. Till I cross the swell-ing tide: Then be-yond this mor-tal shore.

Chorus.

Per-fect rest and peace di-vine.
Lord, I still am trusting Thee.
Trusting Thee with all my power.
I will praise Thee ev-er-more.

Trust-ing Thee whose heart has known Ev-ery care that fills my

This my con-stant joy shall be, That I still am trusting Thee.

own; This my constant joy, my joy shall be, That I still am trusting Thee.

fills my own;

Copyright, 1905, by The Biglow & Main Co.

O BLESSED BIBLE.

FANNY J. CROSBY.　　　　　　　　　　　　　　　FRANK M. DAVIS.

1. O bless-ed, blessed Bi - ble, Our treasured book di - vine, With hope, and joy, and com - fort,
2. Our chart up-on life's o - cean, Our com-fort day by day; The lamp our feet di - rect - ing,
3. Thou tell-est us of Je - sus, The Son of God a - bove, Who came the world to ran - som,
4. O bless - ed, blessed Bi - ble, That God Himself hath given, To fit us for His King-dom

Chorus.

Thy pa - ges bright-ly shine.
The light that guides our way.
So great His won-drous love.
Of end - less life in heaven.

More pre-cious still, than ru - bies, More pure, than purest

gold. Our bless - ed, bless-ed Bi - ble, Thy worth can ne'er be told.

Copyright, 1895, by The Bigelow & Main Co.

118

GATHER THE HARVEST.

Dr. I. L. Mitchell

Frank M. Davis.

1. A - rise and a - way ye reap - ers! The fields of the gold - en corn, Are ripe and ful - ly
2. The gleaners are there be - fore you, The garn - ers are o - pen wide; No time to lose, so
3. Toil on, till the day is o - ver, Too soon will the dark - ness come; The sun is sink - ing

ready for you, Go forth in the ear - ly morn.
has - ten a - way, All day in the field a - bide.
now in the west, Then gath - er the har - vest home.

Chorus.

Press on, press on to gath - er the sheaves, The

work is for you a - lone; Then haste a-way, no time for de - lay, Go gath - er the har - vest home.

Copyright, 1893, by The Biglow & Main Co.

COME JUST NOW!

HARRIET E. JONES.

WILLARD P. MORRIS.

1. O wand'rer come to Je - sus, So long to you a stran - ger, Ac - cept His love, so pre - cious, And leave the path of dan - ger: O come your sins con - fess - ing, Ac - cept the prom-ised bless - ing; O, come in faith, be - liev - ing, And come just now.

2. For - sake each sin - ful pleas - ure, And hold you in His meas - ure, And find the won-drous heal - ing: O come. we en - thralls you. And turn to Him who calls you; O, come in faith, be - liev - ing, And come just now.

3. O come by faith to Je - sus, Law at His foot-stool kneel-ing; lay hold up - on His prom - ise, And ... fa - vor: Leave all that now in - plore you. While an - gels hov - er o'er you; O, come in faith, be - liev - ing, And come just now.

Copyright, 1894, by The Biglow & Main Co.

120

COME, FOLLOW ME.

W. P. M.

W. P. MORRIS.

1. Hear ye the call of the Mas - ter, Sound-ing so full and free; "Like as of
2. Here in His word He in - vit - eth, List to His earn-est plea,— "Leave all the
3. Like - wise the chil-dren He call - eth. "Suf - fer them now," saith He, "For e'en of

Chorus.

"Come, fol - low me." "Come, fol - low me," me, fol-low me,

old, when He called the fish-ers, "Come, fol - low me."
cares of the world be-hind you; "Come, fol - low me,"
such is my heav-'nly kingdom," "Come, fol - low me."

Come, fol - low me"

me, follow me"

Like as of old, when He called the fishers, "Come, follow me."

Copyright, 1895, by The Bigelow & Main Co.

WATCH AND PRAY.

CHARLOTTE ELLIOTT.

A. F. MYERS, arr.

1. Christian seek not yet re - pose, Cast thy dreams of ease a - way; Thou art in the midst of
2. Gird thy heav'n-ly ar - mor on; Near Thee ev - er, night and day Ambushed lies the e - vil
3. Watch, as if on that a - lone Hung the is - sues of the day; Pray that help from heav'n may

Refrain.

foes, Watch and pray,
one, Watch and pray, watch and pray. Watch and pray, be up and do - ing; Ev - 'ry
come, Watch and pray, watch and
pray.

i - dol cast a - way, While the path of life pur - su - ing, Christian pil-grim, watch and pray.

Copyright 1 - by The Bigelow & Main

LIFT UP THE VOICE.

R. L. F. | R. L. FLETCHER.

Copyright, 18[illegible], by The Biglow & Main Co.

LIFT UP THE VOICE.—Concluded.

And tell, O earth, the sto - ry: Our Lord from death a - rose In wondrous might and glo - ry.

COME WITH HAPPY FACES.

F. J. CROSBY. H. P. DANKS.

1. Come with happy fac - es, To the place of pray'r; Je - sus now is wait - ing, We shall find Him there.
2. Come with happy fac - es, Je - sus rose to - day; Leave the world behind us, Seek the narrow way.
3. Come with happy fac - es, Come with hearts sincere; God our tho'ts is read - ing, He is ev - er near.
4. Come with happy fac - es, Learn the words of truth; Je - sus loves the chil-dren; Trust Him in our youth.

Chorus.

With a grateful spir - it, Now our voic-es raise: Thank Him for His goodness, In a song of praise.

Copyright 1899, by The Biglow & Main Co.

ALWAYS CHEERFUL.

124

FANNY J. CROSBY.

REV. ROBERT LOWRY.

1. Let our hearts be always cheerful; Why should murm'ring en-ter there, When our kind and lov-ing Father
2. With His gentle hand to lead us, Should the pow'rs of sin as - sail, He has promised grace to help us;
3. When we turn a side from du - ty, Comes the pain of do-ing wrong; And a shad-ow, creeping o'er us,
4. Oh! the good are al-ways hap-py, And their path is ev - er bright; Let us heed the bless-ed coun-sel,

Refrain.

Makes us chil-dren of His care?
Nev - er can His prom-ise fail.
Checks the rapture of our song.
Shun the wrong and love the right.

Al - ways cheer-ful, al-ways cheer-ful! Sunshine all a -

round we see; Full of beau-ty is the path of du - ty, Cheerful we may al-ways be.

Copyright, 1874, by The Biglow & Main Co.

DO NOT DELAY.

L. E. JONES.

I. H. MEREDITH.

1. Do not de-lay, there is work to be done, On to the harvest where souls may be won, Onward, press onward, the
2. Do not de-lay when the fields are all white, On to the harvest, ere cometh the night, Now is the time, bring the
3. Do not de-lay, for the workers are few, Do not be i-dle, there's plenty to do, Speak to the lost ones in

Chorus.

light fades a-way. Work for the Master while yet it is day. } On - ward, do not de-lay, Work for the
lost wand'rers in. Garnered with joy from the highways of sin. }
ten - derest love, Point them to Je - sus, the Sav-iour a-bove. }

Onward, onward,

Master while yet it is day. On - ward. Do not de-lay, Work for the Master, O has-ten a-way.

Onward, onward.

Copyright 1894 by The Meth. & Main Co.

126

W. A. O.

SOWING THE PRECIOUS SEED.

W. A. OGDEN.

1. Sow-ing the pre-cious seed In the ear - ly dawn of morn - ing, Sow-ing the pre-cious seed
2. Sow-ing the pre-cious seed While the day is fast de - clin - ing, Sow-ing the pre-cious seed
3. Sow-ing the pre-cious seed With an ear - nest true en-deav - or, Sow-ing the pre-cious seed

In the noon - day fair; Sow - ing the pre-cious seed, For the youth-ful heart's a - dorn - ing,
In the twi - light dim; Sow - ing the pre-cious seed, Nei - ther doubt-ing, nor re-pin - ing,
Of the gold - en grain; Sow - ing the pre-cious seed, And the hand with-hold - ing nev - er,

D.S.—Break-ing the bread of life. Tell - ing o'er the gos - pel sto - ry.

Chorus. FINE.

Sow - ing the pre-cious seed With a ten - der care.
Leav-ing it all to God, Trust-ing all to Him,
Pray-ing that God will send. It the sun and rain.

Sow-ing the pre-cious seed

We are

Sow-ing the pre - cious seed In the dear home - land.

Copyright, 1884, by The Biglow & Main Co.

127

SOWING THE PRECIOUS SEED.—Concluded.

D.S.

Scat - ter-ing far and wide with pa-tient, lov - ing hand

Sow-ing the precious seed.

FIND IN CHRIST YOUR REST.

F. M. D.

FRANK M. DAVIS.

1. Ye tempt-ed, troubled, sore-ly tried, By sins and wores op-prest, There is a Rock, a Ref-uge nigh,
2. When waves of sorrow sweep the soul, And life seems all un-blest, When joy and peace are vainly sought,
3. Now, as a weary dove would seek Its native heath and nest, Look up-ward with the eye of faith,

D.S.—O look to God with lov - ing faith,

D.S.

FINE.

Find in Christ your rest.

Come find in Christ your rest. }
Then find in Christ your rest. }
And find in Christ your rest. }

your rest

your rest.

Find in Christ your rest.

And find in Christ your rest.

Used by permission.

O COME, WEARY ONE.

H. N. LINCOLN.

CHAS. EDW. POLLOCK.

1. O come, weary one, to the on-ly sure Refuge, Where mer-cy and pardon are bound-less and free;
2. come, weary one, for the daybeams are fading; Say, why on the des-ert a - far wilt thou roam?
3. come, weary one, for the night-clouds pursue thee; How darkly they frown on the cold mountain's brow;
4. come, weary one. He is urging thee onward; One step o'er the threshold and life thou shalt gain:

O haste with thy burden of sin and of sor-row, Thy gracious Re-deem-er is wait-ing for thee.
The arms of the Saviour will glad-ly enfold thee, He longs with for-give-ness to welcome thee home.
The voice of the tempest is waiting around thee, And none but the Sav-iour can shel - ter thee now.
The light of His love thro' the darkness is breaking; All glo - ry to Je-sus, the Lamb that was slain!

Chorus.

O come, come un - to Him,

Come, come un - to Him,

Where mer - cy and par - don are boundless and free:

Copyright, 1895, by The Biglow & Main Co.

O COME, WEARY ONE.—Concluded.

Haste with thy bur-den of sin and of sor-row, Thy gra-cious Re-deem-er is wait-ing for thee.

HOSANNA TO OUR KING!

J. F. DISNEY.

W. A. OGDEN.

1. This is the day the Lord hath made, O earth re-joice and sing; Let songs of tri-umph
2. The stone the build-ers set at naught Is Zi-on's might-y done: The sure foun-da-tion
3. Christ is the stone re-jec-ted once, And num-bered with the slain: Now raised in glo-ry

D.S.—Zi-on shout a-

FINE. Chorus. D.S.

hail the morn, Ho-san-na to our King!
for our faith, And hope for time to come.
from the dead, E-ter-nal-ly to reign.

Ho-san-na, ho-san-na, Let songs of triumph ring. Let

loud for joy, Ho-san-na to our King!

Copyright, 1895, by The Biglow & Main Co.

DO YOU KNOW THE SONG?

A. P. COBB

J. H. FILLMORE.

1. Do you know the song that the an - gels sang On that night in the long a - go?
2. Do you know the song that the shep-herds heard, As they watch'd o'er their flocks by night?
3. Do you know the story that the wise men learned, As they jour-neyed from the East a - far?

When the heav'ns a - bove with their mu - sic rang, Till it ech-oed in the earth be - low?
When the skies bent down, and their hearts were stirr'd By the voic - es of the an - gels bright?
O'er a path-way plain, for there night - ly burn'd In their sight, a glo-rious guid-ing star.

Chorus.

All glo - ry in the high - est. Peace on earth, good will to men. Glo - ry,

Copyright, 1892, by Fillmore Bros. Used by per.

DO YOU KNOW THE SONG?—Concluded.

glo - ry in the high - est, in the high - est, Glo - ry, glo - ry, glo - ry

in the high - est, Glo - ry in the high - est. Peace on earth, good will to men.

THE LORD'S PRAYER.

THOMAS TALLIS.

Matt. 6: 9-13.

1. Our Father, which art in heaven, Hallowed . . be thy name; { Thy kingdom come, thy will be done in . . earth, as it is in heaven.
2. Give us this day our dai-ly bread. Andforgiveusourdebts,as we for - give our debtors.
3. And lead us not into temptation; but deliver us from evil: { For thine is the king- dom, and the . . power, and the glory, for - ever. A - men.

132
COME, OH COME.

I. H. M.

I. H. MEREDITH.

1. Come, O come, while Christ is call - ing, Ling-er not in paths of sin;
2. Come, O come, while Christ is plead-ing; O what love His tones con-vey;
3. Come, O come, de - lay no long - er, For th' ac-cept - ed time is now;

Sev - er ev - 'ry tie that binds you, And the heav'nly race be - gin.
Will you slight His prof-fered mer - cy, Will you long-er from Him stray?
Yield, oh yield yourself' to Je - sus; And be - fore His scep-tre bow.

Chorus.

Calling now, calling now, Hear the Saviour call - ing now.

Call-ing now, call-ing now, Hear the Saviour call - ing now.

Saviour call-ing now, Call-ing now, call-ing now,
calling now, Calling now, calling now,

Copyright, 1895, by The Biglow & Main Co.

WHO'LL BE FOR JESUS?

Words arr.

W. A. Ogden.

1. Onward! onward! the great com-mand; Who'll be the first to join our band? From the snares of the
2. Onward! onward! the way pur-sue; Go with a heart and courage true. Bear with patience the
3. Onward! onward! the prize is sure; If to the end you shall en - dure. Then at last with the

Chorus.

world, to fly! Taste the joys that will nev-er die
ills you meet, In your heart hide His counsels sweet. } Who'll be for Jesus, who will bear Forth in the
ceased a - bove, Swell the song of re-deem-ing love. }

light His ban-ner fair? Who'll be for Je - sus, who will go With His ar - my, a-gainst the foe?

Copyright, 1895, by The Biglow & Main Co.

134

IN THE CLEFT OF THE ROCK.

W. P. M.

W. A. OGDEN.

1. In the cleft of the Rock, O Sav-iour hide me, There in Thy ho-ly place;
2. In the cleft of the Rock, O Sav-iour keep me, Safe from the tempt-er's power;
3. In the cleft of the Rock, O Sav-iour shield me, E'er from the darts of sin;

When the storm on the sea of life is rag-ing, Hold me by Thy grace.
And by faith let me cling to Thy dear prom-ise, In that ho-ly hour.
From the world and its snares, O keep me ev - er, Lest my heart they win.

Chorus.

In the Rift - ed Rock let me hide.... When dark and storm-y waves round me roll;
let me hide,

Copyright, 1899, by The Biglow & Main Co.

IN THE CLEFT OF THE ROCK.—Concluded.

In the bless-ed Rock I would ev-er-more a-bide; For there is the refuge of my soul.

GOD HEARETH PRAYER.

Rev. R. F. GORDON.

HUBERT P. MAIN.

1. Let not thy heart despair, Nor be a-fraid; God hear-eth earnest pray'r, He giv-eth aid;
2. What tho' mis-for-tunes fall Part of thy lot; They can-not take thine all, God chang-eth not;
3. This earth is not the home, Where thou shalt stay; Here constant changes come, Time speeds a-way;

He is thy helper nigh, And will thy need supply. Then on His love re-ly. Calm un-dis-mayed.
Look up with hope-ful glance, Be of glad count'nance; On-ward in faith advance, Sad-ness for-got.
Yet when life's transient gleam Fades like a pass-ing dream, Brightly on thee will beam An end-less day.

Copyright 1896 by The Hart & Main Co.

136

COMING, YES, WE'RE COMING.

F. J. CROSBY.

W. H. DOANE.

1. How sweet the call of mer-cy, In-vit-ing ev-ery heart To come and love the Sav-iour, Ere
2. O may His Spir-it teach us To know and do the right; To walk as He commands us, That
3. Our Sav-iour loves the chil-dren, On them His hands were laid, With-in His arms He held them, And

youth-ful days de - part; 'Tis in the Ho-ly Bi - ble, These precious words we see: For -
we may see the light; The bless-ed light that shin-eth A - long the nar-row way. And
bless'd them while He prayed; And still His mer-cy calls them, Just now we hear Him say: I

Refrain.

bid ye not the chil-dren, But let them come to Me,
al - ways grow-eth bright-er, Un - to the per-feet day.
want your hearts, dear chil-dren, I want your love to-day,

Com-ing, yes, we're com-ing,

Com-ing, com - ing,

Copyright 1875, by Biglow & Main.

COMING, YES, WE'RE COMING.—Concluded.

Repeat softly.

Com - ing, yes, we're com - ing, Com - ing, yes, we're com - ing, Dear Sav - iour, to Thy fold.

Com - ing,

Com - ing.

I TRUST IN THEE.

JESSIE L. SPORE.

W. A. OGDEN.

1. Sav - iour Thy guid ing hand Ex - tend to me, While on life's fit - ful strand
2. Vain all my ef - forts, Lord, Un - blest by Thee, On Thine e - ter - nal word
3. Thy blood for me was shed, O King di - vine, Thorns crown'd Thy sa - cred head
4. Let all my ac - tions prove My love for Thee, And to Thy home a - bove

My trust in Thee shall be, Sav - iour, Sav - iour, I trust in Thee.
For me O lead Thou me, Sav - iour, Sav - iour, My trust in Thee.
Still Thou shalt mine and Thine, Sav - iour, Sav - iour, For me be mine.
O lead Thou me, Sav - iour, Sav - iour, Still Thou lead me.

Copyright, 18 , by The Biglow & Main Co.

FALL INTO LINE.

Wm. H. Gardner.

Chas. K. Langley.

1. O - ver hill and loft - y mount - ain, Hear the gos - pel trum - pet call,
2. Gird - ing on the roy - al ar - mor, Wave the glo - rious ban - ner high!
3. Sound a - gain the sil - ver trum - pet, Sound a - loud the bat - tle cry!

Lis - ten to the strains in - spir - ing, 'Tis a mes - sage for us all.
While for truth and right con - tend - ing, An - gels watch you from the sky.
"All for Je - sus, all for Je - sus!" We shall con - quer though we die.

Chorus.

Fall in - to line for the con - flict, Fall in - to line for the con - flict,
fall in - to line, fall in - to line,

Copyright, 1903, by The Biglow & Main Co.

FALL INTO LINE.—Concluded.

Ral-ly christian soldiers all.

Ral-ly at the trumpet's call, ral-ly, ral-ly
Ral-ly at the trumpet's call, ral-ly, ral-ly

JESUS, MY ALL.

Scotch Air.

FANNY J. CROSBY.

rit.

1. Lord, at Thy mer-cy-seat, Humb-ly I fall; Pleading Thy promise sweet, Lord, hear my call;
2. Tears of re-pentant grief Si - lent-ly fall; Help thou my un-be-lief, Hear thou my call;
3. Still at Thy mer-cy-seat, Humb-ly I fall; Pleading Thy promise sweet, Heard is my call.

rit.

Now let Thy work be-gin, Oh, make me pure within, Cleanse me from ev - ery sin, Je - sus, my all.
Oh, how I pine for Thee! 'Tis all my hope and plea; Je - sus has died for me, Je - sus, my all.
Faith wings my soul to Thee; This all my hope shall be, Je - sus has died for me, Je - sus, my all.

Used by per.

140

SOMETHING TO DO.

FRANK W. HUTT.

CHAS. H. GABRIEL.

1. Je - sus, our Saviour and Friend, How can we serve Thee to - day? Teach us a life - giv - ing
2. Lord, in Thy goodness and might, Thou hast a bless - ing for all, Help us to lead some poor
3. Lord, in Thy name we would go, Tak - ing Thy prom-ise of love, Un - to the child-ren so

message to send To souls that are go - ing a - stray. Help us to take by the hand, ...
soul to the light, Now falt'ring, and read-y to fall. Help us to take by the hand,
ea - ger to know The joys of Thy kingdom a - bove.

Chorus.

Lost ones, and tell of Thy love, ... Lead them with joy to the heavenly land, Shining in glory a - bove.
Lost ones, and tell of Thy love.

Copyright, 1899, by The Bigelow & Main Co.

WE ARE TOILING ON.

W. A. O.

W. A. OGDEN.

1. We are toil-ing on t'ward the land of rest, To our home a-bove on the shin-ing shore.
2. We are toil-ing on in the nar-row way, And our feet are shod with the gos-pel peace;
3. We are toil-ing on in the pathway bright, Lead-ing up-ward still to our home a-bove.

FINE.

To the Ca-naan fair where a-bide the blest—The re-deemed who have gone be-fore.
By the eye of faith we can see the rays of the morn-ing of our re-lease.
Where the Lamb of God is the bless-ed light, And the ful-ness of joy and love.

D. S.—We are toil-ing on t'ward the land of rest, To our home on the shin-ing shore.

Chorus.

Toil-ing on, ... toil-ing on, ... Toil-ing on, ... toil-ing on,

On, ... toil-ing on, ... toil-ing on,

Toil-ing on, toil-ing on, Toil-ing on, ... toil-ing on,

D. S.

Copyright 1895, by The Fillmore & Main Co.

142

W. P. M.

TO THE WORK, ONE AND ALL.

GEO. C. HUGG.

1. To the work, one and all, let the call re-sound! To the work, one and all, let the
2. To the work, one and all, with a will-ing hand! Send the word of life o - ver the
3. To the work, one and all, let the chil-dren hear! Tell the won - drous love of the

word go round; If to reap, or to sow, you His love would show, Go forth in Je - sus' name.
all the land. To the sons of men speak the word a - gain, Go forth in Je - sus' name.
Sav - iour dear; Bring them in to - day from the broad highway; Go forth in Je - sus' name.

Chorus.

La-bor on, La-bor on, la - bor on, la - bor on, In the vine-yard of the Lord la - bor on,

Copyright, 1895, by The Bigelow & Main Co.

TO THE WORK, ONE AND ALL.—Concluded.

Labor on, Labor on,
la-bor on, la-bor on,
And thy toil He shall reward.
re-ward.

SPEAK JUST A WORD FOR JESUS.

WILLARD P. MORRIS.

I. D. K.

1. Tell what the Lord has done for you, Speak just a word for Je-sus! Stand for the right, be
2. Ear-ly be-gin to bear the cross, Speak just a word for Je-sus! They who de-ny Him
3. Fear not the world, its sneer or frown, Speak just a word for Je-sus! They who en-dure, shall

firm and true, Speak just a word for Je-sus!—Just a word, just a word. Just a word for Je-sus.
suf-fer loss, Speak just a word for Je-sus!—Just a word, just a word. Just a word for Je-sus.
wear the crown, Speak just a word for Je-sus!—Just a word, just a word. Just a word for Je-sus.

Copyright, 1897, by The Biglow & Main Co.

144

THEY SING A NEW SONG.

JULIA H. JOHNSTON.

P. BILHORN.

1. High in yonder heav'nly courts the ransomed sing, Cast-ing down their golden crowns before their King;
2. Oh, the wondrous song of Love, at last com-plete! Oh, the gold-en vi - als, full of o - dors sweet;
3. On-ly those whose robes are washed, can join that throng, None but lips attuned by grace can sing that song:

I am-ished every grief and fear and earth-ly wrong, While the saints redeemed now join the glad new song.
Thro' the ris-en Saviour, once for sin - ners slain, We as kings and priests to God shall ev-er reign.
Cleanse us, blessed Saviour from the stain of sin, Let the glo-rious song of rapt-ure now be - gin!

Chorus.

Sing - - ing to the Lamb . . . . . who once was slain on Cal - va - ry:
Singing to the Lamb, slain on Cal - va - ry, Cal-va-ry;

Sing-ing to the Lamb,

Copyright, 1891, by P. Bilhorn. Used by per.

THEY SING A NEW SONG.—Concluded.

Sing . . . ing to the Lamb, Who ev-er lives e-ter-nal-ly.
Sing-ing to the Lamb,
Sing-ing to the Lamb,

WHO AT MY DOOR IS STANDING?

Mrs. M. B. C. SLADE.   Dr. A. B. EVERETT.

1. Who at my door is stand-ing, Pa-tient-ly draw-ing near, Entrance within de-mand-ing?
2. Lone-ly with-out He's stay-ing, Lone-ly with-in am I; While I am still de-lay-ing,
3. All thro' the dark hours drear-y, Knock-ing a-gain is He; Je-sus, art Thou not wea-ry
4. Door of my heart, I hast-en Quick-ly to o-pen wide; Tho' He re-buke and chas-ten,

D.S.—If Thou wilt heed My call-ing.

FINE.   Refrain.

Whose voice is this I hear?
Will He not pass me by?
Wait-ing so long for me?
He will with me a-bide.

Sweet-ly the tones are fall-ing:— "O-pen the door for Me!"

D.S.

I will a-bide with Thee.

Copyright of R. M. McIntosh.

146

THE BELLS ARE RINGING.

WM. H. GARDNER.

FRANK M. DAVIS

1. The bells are ring-ing sweet-ly, From ma-ny a steep-le tower; They hail the New Year's
2. They tell of Gods great good-ness, To all the sons of men; How He is ev - er
3. They tell of gold - en sun-shine, That com - eth with the Spring; Of smil - ing skies in
4. They tell of those de-part - ed, To yon - der bliss - ful shore; Where we, some day, shall

Chorus.

com - ing, At midnight's sol - emn hour.
read - y, To bless them yet a - gain. Ring out a song of glad - ness, Ring out a
beau - ty, That sum-mer days will bring;
meet them, When life's brief work is o'er.

ring,

song of peace, . . . Be-hold! the time is com - ing When grief and care shall ceas . .
a song of peace,

Copyright, 1895, by The Bigelow & Main Co.

BANNER OF THE LORD.

JENNIE WILSON.

WILLARD P. MORRIS.

1. It is a roy - al ban - ner, O Christians that ye bear; Guard well that ho-ly stand-ard,
2. The Lord His en - sign giv - eth, To those who fear His name. An em-blem of His mer - cy,
3. Un - sul - lied keep this ban - ner, Let naught its brightness mar; That souls in darkness dwell - ing,
4. Thro' wea-ri-ness and con - flict Your banner bear in faith; As - sured that your Re-deem - er

Chorus.

Com - mit - ted to your care.
Sal - va - tion to pro-claim.
May see its gleam a - far.
Will con-quer sin and death.

How glorious is the ban - ner, The ban-ner of the Lord!

O Christians, guard from ev-ery ill, Watch o'er, protect, defend it still, The ban-ner of the Lord.

Copyright, 1896, by The Biglow & Main Co

A HAPPY NEW YEAR!

FANNY J. CROSBY.

W. P. MORRIS.

1. The New Year has come like a child in its glee, And wonders, perhaps, what its greeting may be
2. How kind-ly our Saviour, and Shepherd a-bove, Has sheltered His flock in the arms of His love,
3. Oh, let us be grateful for blessings like these, And try from this moment our Saviour to please;

It comes like a sunbeam our pathway to cheer; 'Then sing we to-geth-er a Happy New Year!
How rich-ly His goodness and mercy are spread, Each day o'er our pathway as on-ward we're led.
To serve Him more faithful, and love Him more dear, Be - gin on the morn of this Happy New Year.

Chorus.

Our Pas - tor, our Teachers, our Par-ents so dear, We child-ren all wish you A Hap-py New Year!

Copyright, 1896, by The Biglow & Main Co.

GIRD ON THE ROYAL ARMOR.

GRACE J. FRANCES.

HUBERT P. MAIN.

1. Gird on the roy-al ar-mor; Go forth in Je-sus' name; To those who sit in
2. Lift up the roy-al stand-ard; Go forth our cause to win; With hel-met, shield, and
3. With righteousness our breast-plate, The Spir-it's sword in hand, Still con-q'ring and to

Chorus.

dark - ness The Light of Life pro-claim.
buck - ler, A - gainst the hosts of sin.   Gird on the roy - al ar - mor, That
con - quer, Press on at God's com-mand.

we the foe may face, And trust-ing our Com-mand - er, Be vic - tors thro' His grace.

Copyright, 1890, by the Biglow & Main Co.

150

WOODLAND WAYS.

E. E. HEWITT.

GEO. C. HUGG.

FINE.

1. Woodland ways are ringing, Birds are gai-ly sing-ing, Earth is radiant with the smiles of June:
2. Prais-es to our Father, In His house we gath-er, Bringing hymns of grat-i-tude and love:
3. Come with ad-o-ra-tion, For the great sal-va-tion, Bow-ing at our Sav-iour's cross to-day;

Na-ture now re-joic-es, Mingling hap-py voi-ces, Let us, to her notes, our hearts at-tune.
For the hand that guides us, Day by day pro-vides us, Still with blessings sent us from a-bove.
Here in love He meets us, Ten-der-ly He greets us, Leads us on in wis-dom's pleasant way.

Chorus.

D.S.—Join the swell-ing cho-rus, Love is watch-ing o'er us, Fr er-last-ing grace and mer-cy sing.

D.S.

Come with grateful song, Hap-ly praise pro-long, While a-far the woodland ech-oes ring:

Copyright 1894, by Geo. C. Hugg. Used by per.

BELIEVE AND RECEIVE.

151

J. WARD CHILDS.

GEO. C. STEBBINS.

1. Be-lieve and re-ceive the Sav - iour, God's gift of love di - vine, And Christ, and
2. Be-lieve and re-ceive the Sav - iour, For you His blood was shed, He took your
3. Be-lieve and re-ceive the Sav - iour, And ne'er from Him de - part; He'll set His
4. Be-lieve and re-ceive the Sav - iour, Forth to the con - flict go, With the word, the
5. Go forth in the Spir - it's pow - er, And the all pre-vail-ing name Of Christ the

Chorus.

heav-en and glo - ry Shall ev - er-more be thine.
sins up - on Him, And suf - fered in your stead.
mark in your fore-head, His seal up - on your heart.
sword of the Spir - it To meet the ad-vanc-ing foe.
world's re - deem - er, His Gos - pel to pro - claim.

Be - lieve . . . and re-ceive Him, 'Tis

be-lieve

ritard.

all that you have to do; For He, your great Re-deem - er Has done all the rest for you.

Copyright, 1895, by The Biglow & Main Co.

IN THE SHADOW OF THE CROSS.

Dr. I. L. MITCHELL.

W. A. OGDEN.

152

1. Let the war-fare now be-gin, Let us brave the hosts of sin, O the souls that we may win
2. Now the Mas-ter's call o-bey, Souls are dy-ing ev-er-y day; They are drift-ing far a-way
3. Gold-en days are pass-ing by; From the way-side, voi-ces cry, Oh, to save them let us try,

In the shad-ow of the cross, In the darkness of despair Hearts are fail-ing ev-er-y-where,
From the shad-ow of the cross; They are go-ing out to sea, From their per-il set them free,
In the shad-ow of the cross; Giv-ing suc-cor to the weak, Words of cheer and com-fort speak,

Chorus.

For the strug-gle now pre-pare, In the shad-ow of the cross; In the shad - ow of the
Bid them now for ref-uge flee To the shad-ow of the cross.
Guide them to the home they seek In the shad-ow of the cross.

In the shadow

Copyright Prop. by The Biglow & Main Co.

IN THE SHADOW OF THE CROSS.—Concluded.

We will set the bea - con light.

That shall nev - er suf - fer loss

We shall never suf - fer loss, suf-fer loss,

cross . . . . That shall nev - . .

of the cross

Flash the sig - nal clear and bright, In the shad-ow of the cross.

HE PRAYETH BEST.

W P M

C T C

1 { He prayeth best who loveth best, both man and bird and beast.
   { For he hath of-fered to the Lord Omit

2 { He prayeth best who loveth best, All things, both great and small,
   { For He, our Lord who loveth us, Omit

Who giv-eth to the beast.

Hath made and loves them all.

154 AWAY, AWAY WITH THE WORD OF LIFE. Missionary.

Rev. M. L. HOFFORD.

W. A. OGDEN.

1. A - way, a - way o'er the o-cean wave, A - way to the wood-land deep; A - way, a - way to the
2. A - way, a - way with a bounding heart, A - way with a flam-ing tongue; A - way, a-way where the
3. A - way, a - way to the glorious work, A - way with the dawning bright; A - way, a - way with a

west-ern wilds Where boundless prairies sweep. At the Master's ear-nest call. To the work we glad-ly
tid - ings sweet Of grace were nev - er sung, With the "Word of God" a-way; With its precious promise
zeal that makes The cross a bur - den light; In the home, and by the way. There the seed of truth to

Chorus.

go; From morning light 'till the evening shade, The seeds of truth to sow.
giv'n, A - way, a - way to re-claim the lost, And point them up to heav'n. } A - way o'er the o - cean
sow; The des-ert then shall rejoice and bloom, And His sal - va - tion know.

Used by per. of W. A. Ogden, owner of copyright.

AWAY, AWAY WITH THE WORD OF LIFE.—Concluded.

wave, A-way to the woodland deep, A-way, a-way with the "Word of Life" where boundless prairies sweep.

IN THE GOSPEL FIELD.

E. A. BARNES.

E. T. POUND.

1. Work-ers in the gos-pel field, Toil-ing for the Lord, Would you make the foe to yield?
2. Work-ers in the gos-pel field, Speed His cause a - long, Let Him be your Strength and Shield,
3. Work-ers in the gos-pel field, Do not yet re - pine; La - bor that His foes may yield,

D. S.—Go and la - bor while you may,

FINE.

Trust the Sav-iour's word }
And your hap - py song } In the gos - pel field,
Trust His pow'r di - vine. } O la - bor,

Chorus.

In the gos - pel field.

D. S.

In the gos - pel field.

156

THE SAVIOUR CHRIST IS BORN!

W. O. CUSHING.

W. A. OGDEN.

1. Hail the joy-ful tid-ings, Christ the King is born! Earth and heav'n rejoicing, Crown this welcome morn!
2. Ho! ye wondrous shepherds On Ju-de-a's plain, Shout the joy-ful tidings, Je-sus comes to reign!
3. Joy to ev-ery na-tion! "Peace, good will to men"! Sound the joy-ful anthem. Wake the song a-gain!

Her-ald an-gels bend-ing From the star-ry fold, Chant-ing joy-ful anthems, Strike their
Watching for the morn-ing, Wait-ing for the day,— Hark! the an-gel cho-rus, "Christ is
Send a-broad the ti-dings! Bear it far a-way: Joy to ev-ery na-tion. "Christ is

Chorus. DUET. *obligato.*

Glo - ry! glo - ry!

Glo - ry to God in the high - - est! All hail the wel-come

Glo - ry to God!

Glo - ry to God!

harps of gold.
born to day.
born to day.

* This chorus is complete without the duet obligato; but much more effective with it

Copyright 1895 by The Bigow & Main Co.

THE SAVIOUR, CHRIST IS BORN.—Concluded.

Glo - ry to God!

Glo - ry to God!

morn'

Glo - ry to God!
Glo - ry to God!

Glo - ry to God!

on the high - - est! The Sav-iour, Christ is born.

Glo - ry to God!

LIST! THE GLAD SONG.

FRANZ GRUBER.

MARIA STRAUB, per.

1. List! the glad song, beauti-ful song, God is love, God is love. Hear the voices for - ev - er they tell,
2. Hear the soft breeze, whispering breeze, Sigh and swell, sweetly tell, In a murmuring mel - o - dy sweet
3. Now the birds sing, joy-ful-ly sing, God is love, God is love, Hark the mel-o-dy float-eth a-way

Soft - ly, gently, the ech-oes swell, Whispering God is love, Whispering God is love,
They the sto-ry so softly re-peat Whispering God is love, Whispering God is love.
On the wings of the morn-ing gay, Whispering God is love, Whispering God is love.

158

HAIL! PRINCE OF PEACE.

LAURA E. NEWELL.

WILLARD P. MORRIS.

1. Hail! Prince of Peace, all hail! Ac - cept our love and praise. We greet Thy ad - vent to the earth
2. Hail! Prince of Peace, all hail! Oh, rule in ev - ery heart! Un - to each soul be - fore Thee now,
3. Hail! Prince of Peace, all hail! Wilt Thou with us a - bide? Oh, star of hope beam on our way,

DUET.

With glad har - mo - nious lays. We on this Christ-mas day Would raise each tune-ful voice,
Wilt Thou Thy grace im-part. With rap-tured hosts in heav'n That sing on Beth'hem's plain,
Be 'Thou our strength and guide, Our an-thems, love in-spired, In con-cert now we sing;

Chorus.

To welcome Thee, blest Prince of Peace, Let all in Thee re - joice! }
We'd sound the tid-ings of Thy birth In one sub-lime re - frain. } Hail! Prince of Peace all hail!
Praise shall not cease, blest Prince of Peace, For Thou art Lord and King!

Copyright, 1898, by The Biglow & Main Co.

HAIL! PRINCE OF PEACE.—Concluded.

All hail! our Sovereign King! We at Thy feet would humbly bow, And grateful off'rings bring

HEAR ME, BLESSED JESUS.

F. J. C.

J. H. BURKE.

1. Hear me, blessed Je - sus, Bid all fear de - part; Let Thy Spir-it whis-per Peace within my heart.
2. Let me ful - ly trust Thee, Resting on Thy word; Let me still with patience Wait on Thee, O Lord.
3. Hid - ing in the shad-ow Of Thy shel'ring wings, I shall rest con-fid - ing In the King of kings.

Chorus.

Then, whate'er Thou sendest, Happy shall I be, Je - sus, my Re-deem-er, Look-ing un - to Thee.

Copyright, 1891, by The Biglow & Main Co.

HOME, GATHERING HOME.

W. A. O.

W. A. OGDEN.

1. Shall we gath - er in His King-dom, you and I,
2. Shall the bless - ed Sav - iour greet us on that shore,
3. Shall our voi - ces swell the tri-umph-ant song,

gath - er by and by? In that shore?
greet us on that triumph-ant song; Where
glad, tri-umph-ant song, With

that hap - py land be - yond the star - ry sky,
is sor - row, and is sigh - ing nev - er - more.
the blood - re-deemed, the great and might - y throng,

Gath - er by and by,
Greet us on that shore,
Glad, tri-umph-ant song.

Chorus.

Home, ... gath-'ring home, ...

Home, we're gath-'ring home, gath-'ring home.

O say, shall we meet o - ver there?
O say, shall we meet o - ver there?
O say, shall we meet o - ver there?

Copyright, 1895, by The Biglow & Main Co.

HOME, GATHERING HOME.—Concluded.

Gath'ring home. . . . gath'ring home, ... home to our friends o-ver there. . . .

Home, gath'ring home, home, gath'ring home, o-ver there.

ONE BY ONE.

S. ANNA GORDON.

W. P. MORRIS.

1. One by one, God takes them. The jew - els all His own. From all cor-rod-ing
2. One by one, God claims them, The buds of life's young spring; To bloom in heav'n-ly
3. One by one, God calls them, By some new heav'n-ly name. That in the man-sion

cares of earth To thine e - ter - nal home.
jew - a - ces, The courts of Christ, their King.
of the blest, O'er cher-ished ones may claim.

1 One by one, we miss them,
And mourn their absence here;
As one, by one, God calls them
And wipes the falling tear.

5 One by one, God takes them
Beyond the river's flow,
And one by one with silent steps,
To fairer climes they go.

Copyright, 1891, by The Biglow & Main Co.

WE'LL MEET IN THE MORNING.

E. E. Hewitt.

Chas. Edw. Prior.

1. We part for a lit-tle, but partings will ease, We'll meet by the riv-er in mansions of peace,
2. The bonds of af-fec-tion u - nit - ed in Him, Are grow-ing with lus-tre no a - ges can dim.
3. We part for a little, we whisper "good night," And then comes the dawning all glorious and bright,

With sadness and weeping we whisper "good night," But soon dawns the morning of fade-less de-light.
They can-not be bro-ken by death's ruthless hand; To - geth - er with Je - sus, re-joic-ing we'll stand.
When gather'd in glad-ness on Fair E-den's shore. We'll join in the an-them of peace ev - er-more.

Chorus.

We'll meet in the morning, the clouds rolled away, We'll meet in the morning of heav'ns glorious day;

Copyright, 1-9, by The Biglow & Main Co.

WE'LL MEET IN THE MORNING.—Concluded.

Then trust-ful-ly, hope ful-ly, whisper "good night," "We'll meet in the morning, and all will be right.

HE GIVETH HIS BELOVED SLEEP.

LAURA E. NEWELL.

D. W. CRIST.

1. He giv - eth His be - lov - ed sleep. He notes when wea - ry grows the way;
2. He dries their tears so ten - der - ly; With lov - ing voice He leads them home,
3. Then cease thy grief, for sweet their sleep, Who slum - ber on the Sav-iour's breast,
4. O prom - ise of e - ter - nal rest, Where none their wea - ry vig - ils keep,

And gent - ly then they close their eyes, To o - pen in e - ter - nal day.
And past life's rug - ged, thorn - y way; In fields of joy they ev - er roam.
In yon - der home they ne'er shall weep, He giv - eth His be - lov - ed rest.
We too, shall dwell a - mong the blest, No more to sor - row, or to weep.

Copyright 1896 by D. W. Crist. Used by per.

LIGHT IN THE TOMB.

JENNIE WILSON.

JAS. L. ORR.

1. Hal-le-lu-jah! rejoice, for the Sav-iour is ris-en, From the grave He has banished the gloom;
2. Hal-le-lu-jah! the sway of the death-king is broken, He no long-er in tri-umph shall reign;
3. Hal-le-lu-jah! all glo-ry and hon-or to Je-sus, For the brightness that shines from the tomb;

He has o-pened the por-tals of death's lonely prison, There is light, ho-ly light in the tomb.
Christ is ris-en, and left us a glo-ri-ous to-ken, From the grave we shall rise up a-gain.
From its thralldom He came in His might, to re-lease us, And with hope its dark shade to il-lume.

Chorus.

There is light, ho-ly light, There is light ho-ly light in the tomb!
There is light, There is light, ho-ly light,

Copyright, 1895, by The Biglow & Main Co.

LIGHT IN THE TOMB.—Concluded.

Let the sym-bol of life, lil-ies fair, sweet-ly bloom, There is light, ho-ly light in the tomb.

YOUNG MEN AND MAIDENS.

W. P. MORRIS.

W. P. M.

1. Young men and maid-ens, Praise ye the Lord! Trust and re-ly ye up-
2. Young men and maid-ens, Praise ye the Lord! He ma-ny bless-ings on
3. Young men and maid-ens, Hear ye His call, Hear ye the word of the

on His word; Round and a-bout you His ar-mor gird.—Forth to the con-flict go!
you hath poured, Now for the Mas-ter, draw the sword.—Forth to the con-flict go!
Lord of all, Stand for the truth, and the foe shall fall, Forth to the con-flict go!

166

SWEET THE BELLS ARE RINGING.

J. A. S.

J. A. SHANNON.

1. Sweet the bells are ring-ing On this Eas-ter day; To the world they're sing-ing,
2. Mes-sage of such glad-ness, Ring it out a-gain, Ring a-way all sad-ness,
3. Eas-ter bells for-ev-er Ring the sto-ry sweet, Un-til all the na-tions

Refrain.

Solo.
What is it they say?
Ring a-way all pain.
Bow at Je-sus' feet.

Chorus.

Tutti. Hal-le-lu-jah! Christ is ris-en, Hear the glad bells say,

Solo. Hal-le-lu-jah! Christ is ris-en,

Tutti. Hal-le-lu-jah! Christ is ris'n to-day! Hal-le-lu-jah! Christ is ris-en,

Chorus.

Tutti. He is ris'n

Copyright, 1899 by The Biglow & Main Co.

SWEET THE BELLS ARE RINGING.—Concluded.

Chorus.

He is ris'n in - deed, You will find in Him The ve - ry Friend you need

HE LIVES, OUR RISEN KING.

ALEXCENAH THOMAS.

J. H. KURZENKNABE.

Fine.

1. Joy, Joy, Joy. He lives our ris-en King: Joy, Joy, Joy, Let men and angels sing. The night of death is
2. Joy, Joy, Joy, In every heart abound: Joy, Joy, Joy, O'er all the earth resound. He comes with might and

D.C.—Joy, Joy, Joy. He lives our ris-en King: Joy, Joy, Joy. Let men and angels sing.

D.C.

scattered, All men may life obtain. The gloomy pris-on shattered And Je-sus comes to reign.
pow - er, The Lord of light and love, He lives, He lives to save us, He reigns in heav'n a - bove.

Copyright by J. H. Kurzenknabe.

BRIGHT DAY OF FLOWERS.

ELLEN C. WEBSTER.

J. H. TENNEY.

1. We hail this hap-py day of flowers, The bells and buds we bring;
2. We thank Thee, Lord, that win-ters chill Has pass'd from earth a-way;
3. In morn of life, our hearts we bring To Him, the Lord of love.

The best that bloom in sun-ny bow-ers, To glo-ri-fy our King.
His name we praise for birds that trill Bright songs in sum-mer day.
And hal-le-lu-jah's we will sing To God who reigns a-bove.

Chorus.

Bright day of flowers, ... bright day of flowers, We'll glad-ly join and sing
Bright day of flowers, bright day of flowers,

Copyright, 1880, by The Bigelow & Main Co.

BRIGHT DAY OF FLOWERS. Concluded.

The sweetest lays of grateful praise. To Christ, the children's King.

The sweetest lays, grateful praise the children's King.

THE LOVE OF GOD.

W. A. O.

1. From the throne of God is streaming, Love so free, Love so free, And 'tis of-fered to the
2. When a cap-tive, Je-sus sought me, Set me free, Set me free, By His blood He saved and
3. Now re-deemed, I'll tell the sto-ry, "Grace is free," Grace is free, Un-to Christ be all the

D. S.—Thee, His grace and ten - der

FINE. Chorus.

sin - ner, E - ven un - to me
brought me His own child to be   Love di-vine, so full and free, Shown by Christ on Calva-ry
glo - ry, For He res-cued me.

D. S.

mer-cy. He hath res - cued me.

Copyright, 1889, by The Bigelow & Main Co.

SONG OF THE REDEEMED.

ANNA J. GRANNIS.

W. A. OGDEN.

1. In the might-y sweep of an - gel - ic harps, There's an un - re - spon - sive string;
2. There's a joy the an - gels can nev - er share, While the end - less a - ges roll;
3. There's a sto - ry true, an - gels can - not tell, Who have lived with God in heav'n;

But the note which an - gels can - not make, The re-deem'd of the Lord can sing.
Ex'n the joy of one who's been re-deem'd, The joy of the ran-somed soul.
'Tis the sto - ry sweet they a - lone can tell, Who have sinned and have been for - given.

Chorus.

Shall we sing it to-geth-er, you and I? (you and I?) With the wond'ring an-gels-standing by; . .
Shall we share it to-geth-er, you and I? (you and I?)
Shall we tell it to-geth-er, you and I? (you and I?) With the wond'ring an - gels stand-ing by;

Copyright, 1895, by The Bigelow & Main Co.

SONG OF THE REDEEMED.—Concluded.

shall we sing it out in the courts a - bove, That heav'n is ours through re-deem-ing love?

171 BEAUTIFUL RIVER.
Tune—(. H. 1 *, No. (6,).)

1 Shall we gather at the river,
Where bright angel feet have
trod—
With its crystal tide, forever
Flowing from the throne of God?

CHORUS.

Yes, we'll gather at the river,
The beautiful, the beautiful river—
Gather with the saints at the river,
That flows by the throne of God.

2 On the margin of the river,
Washing up its silver spray,
We will walk and worship ever
All the happy, golden day.

3 Soon we'll reach the shining river,
Soon our pilgrimage will cease:
Soon our happy hearts will quiver
With the melody of peace.
B. Lowry.

172 NEAR THE CROSS.
(Tune—(. H. 5, No. 152.)

1 Jesus, keep me near the cross,
There a precious fountain,
Free to all, a healing stream,
Flows from Calvary's mountain.

CHORUS.

In the Cross, in the Cross
Be my glory ever,
Till my raptured soul shall find
Rest beyond the river.

2 Near the Cross! oh, Lamb of God,
Bring its scenes before me;
Help me walk from day to day
With its shadow o'er me.

3 Near the cross I'll watch and wait,
Hoping, trusting ever,
Till I reach the golden strand
Just beyond the river.
Copyright.   Fanny J. Crosby.

173 WE PRAISE THEE.
Tune—G. H. , No. 152.

1 We praise Thee, O God, for the Son
of Thy love,
For Jesus who died, and is now
gone above.

CHORUS.

Hallelujah! Thine the glory;
Hallelujah! Amen;
Hallelujah! Thine the glory; re-
vive us again.

2 We praise Thee, O God, for Thy
Spirit of light,
Who has shown us our Saviour,
and scattered our night.

3 All glory and praise to the Lamb
that was slain,
Who has borne all our sins, and
hath cleansed every stain.

4 Revive us again; fill each heart
with Thy love:
May each soul be rekindled with
fire from above.
W. P. MacKay.

THERE'S A BLESSING FOR ME.

Henrietta E. Blair.

W. J. Kirkpatrick, by per.

1. There is perfect cleansing in the precious blood That flows for all so free, There is
2. I am saved each moment thro' the cleansing blood That now, by faith, I see; I am
3. Oh, the blood that keeps me from the pow'r of sin My constant theme shall be; I have
4. There is life e-ter-nal in the precious blood That still is flow-ing free. And my

full sal-va-tion in its crim-son flood; There's a blessing from the Lord for me.
sweet-ly rest-ing at the cross I love; There's a blessing from the Lord for me.
laid my burden at the Sav-iour's feet; There's a blessing from the Lord for me.
soul shall glo-ry in the Sav-iour's cross; There's a blessing from the Lord for me.

Chorus.

There's a blessing for me, There's a blessing for me, A blessing from the Lord for me;
for me.

There is full sal - va - tion in the crim - son flood; There's a blessing from the Lord for me.

175 WHAT A FRIEND WE HAVE.

(Tune—G. H. 5, No. 162.)

1 What a Friend we have in Jesus,
    All our sins and griefs to bear!
  What a privilege to carry
    Everything to God in prayer!
  Oh, what peace we often forfeit,
    Oh, what needless pains we
      bear—
  All because we do not carry
    Everything to God in prayer!

2 Have we trials and temptations?
    Is there trouble anywhere?
  We should never be discouraged:
    Take it to the Lord in prayer.
  Can we find a Friend so faithful,
    Who will all our sorrows share?
  Jesus knows our every weakness—
    Take it to the Lord in prayer.

176 STAND UP FOR JESUS.

(Tune—G. H. 6, No. 227.)

1 Stand up! stand up for Jesus!
    Ye soldiers of the cross;
  Lift high His royal banner,
    It must not suffer loss;
  From vict'ry unto vict'ry
    His army shall He lead,
  Till every foe is vanquished,
    And Christ is Lord indeed.

2 Stand up! stand up for Jesus!
    The trumpet call obey;
  Forth to the mighty conflict
    In this His glorious day!
  Ye that are men, now serve Him,
    Against unnumbered foes;
  Let courage rise with danger,
    And strength to strength oppose.

177 WORK FOR THE NIGHT.

(Tune—G. H. 6, No. 225.)

1 Work, for the night is coming!
    Work thro' the morning hours;
  Work while the dew is sparkling,
    Work, 'mid springing flowers;
  Work, when the day grows brighter,
    Work, in the glowing sun;
  Work, for the night is coming,
    When man's work is done.

2 Work, for the night is coming!
    Work, thro' the sunny noon;
  Fill brightest hours with labor,
    Rest comes sure and soon.
  Give every flying minute
    Something to keep in store;
  Work, for the night is coming,
    When man works no more.

A GLORIOUS DAWNING.

S. L. CUTHBERT.
J. L. ORR.

1. When the misty clouds around you Hide the sunlight from your eyes, And the darkness that surrounds you
2. Tho' there's darkness here about you, Yon-der shines the cit-y bright; On its streets are those who love you,
3. With His presence ev-er near you, Promised aid and hope to bring, How His words should always cheer you,

Veils the brightness of the skies, Then whene'er your courage falters, Hear the words the Mas-ter said.
Hap-py in its radiant light, With the Sav-iour close be-side you, Do not fear, or be dismayed;
Make your heart with joy to sing, Oh, the light of day is shin-ing, Far beyond the clouds and shade!

Chorus.

When He walked upon the wa-ters, "It is I, be not a-fraid." By and by . . will come the
With His hand and voice to guide you, "It iz I, be not a-fraid." By and by will come the
No more sad-ness or re-pin-ing, "It is I, be not a-fraid."

Copyright, by J. L. Orr. Used by per.

dawn - - ing, Of a glo - rious, hap - py day In the
dawn-ing, come the dawning. Of a glo-rions hap-py day, hap-py day;

bright - ness of the morn - ing. All the clouds . . shall roll a - way
In the brightness of the morning, of the morning. All the clouds shall roll away, fade away

---

1709   HE LEADETH ME.
(Tune—G. H. 5-6, No. 48.)

1 He leadeth me! O blessed thought!
  O words with heavenly comfort fraught!
  Whate'er I do, where'er I be,[tune.
  Still 'tis God's hand that leadeth

REFRAIN.

He leadeth me, He leadeth me,
By His own hand He leadeth me;
His faithful follower I would be,
For by His hand He leadeth me.

2 Lord, I would clasp Thy hand in mine,
  Nor ever murmur nor repine—
  Content whatever lot I see,
  Since 'tis my God that leadeth me.
                    J. H. Gilmore.

1710   DENNIS, S. M.
(Tune—G. H. 5-6, No. 216.)

1 Blest be the tie that binds
  Our hearts in Christian love;
  The fellowship of kindred minds
  Is like to that above.

2 Before our Father's throne
  We pour our ardent prayers;
  Our fears, our hopes, our aims are one,
  Our comforts and our cares.

3 We share our mutual woes,
  Our mutual burdens bear,
  And often for each other flows
  The sympathizing tear.
                    J. Fawcett.

171   AMERICA.
Tune—G. H. 5-6, No. 234.

1 My country, 'tis of thee
  Sweet land of liberty,
  Of thee I sing;
  Land where my fathers died,
  Land of the pilgrims pride
  From every mountain side
  Let freedom ring.

2 Our father's God, to Thee,
  Author of liberty,
  To Thee we sing;
  Long may our land be bright
  With freedom's holy light;
  Protect us by Thy might,
  Great God, our King.
                    S. F. Smith.

SHOW ME THY WAY.

Ida Scott Taylor.

W. A. Ogden.

1. Lord, in my helplessness Come I to Thee; Thou art com-passionate, Hark-en to me!
2. Trav'ling life's wilder-ness, Batt'ling with sin; Fight-ing a-gainst the foe, Vic-t'ry to win;
3. Doubts may entan-gle me, Troubles an - noy; Thou art my comfort-er, Thou art my joy;
4. Help me to cling to Thee, Sav - iour of all; Hear Thou my earnest plea, Lord when I call;

Oh, let me follow Thee, Hum-bly I pray; Lead me, Thou blessed One, Show me Thy way.
Guide me, and strengthen me, Lest I should stray; Sav - iour all - mer-ci - ful, Show me Thy way.
Though I may fal-ter here, Shrink with dismay, Make Thou my choices, Lord, Show me Thy way.
With Thy Al-mighty hand Guard me I pray, Gra-cious-ly, ten-der-ly Show me Thy way.

Refrain.

Show me Thy way. Show me Thy way. Help me in meekness To trust, and o - bey;

Show me Thy way. Show me Thy way.

Copyright, 1895, by The Biglow & Main Co.

SHOW ME THY WAY.—Concluded.

Oh! keep me near to Thee, Thine may I ev-er be; Pa-tient-ly, lov-ing-ly, Show me Thy way.

RESCUE THE PERISHING.
(Tune—G. H. 2-o, No. 17o.)

1 Rescue the perishing,
Care for the dying,
Snatch them in pity from sin and the grave;
Weep o'er the erring one,
Lift up the fallen,
Tell them of Jesus, the mighty to save.

CHORUS.
Rescue the perishing,
Care for the dying;
Jesus is merciful,
Jesus will save.

2 Though they are slighting Him,
Still He is waiting,
Waiting the penitent child to receive;
Plead with them earnestly,
Plead with them gently,
He will forgive if they only believe.

Touched by a loving heart,
Wakened by kindness,
Chords that were broken will vibrate once more.

Fanny J. Crosby.
Copyright.

I HEAR THY WELCOME VOICE.
(Tune—G. H. 5, No. 174.)

1 I hear Thy welcome voice,
That calls me, Lord, to Thee,
For cleansing in Thy precious blood
That flowed on Calvary.

CHORUS.
I am coming, Lord!
Coming, now, to Thee!
Wash me, cleanse me, in the blood
That flow'd on Calvary.

2 Tho' coming weak and vile,
Thou dost my strength assure;
Thou dost my vileness fully cleanse,
Till spotless all and pure.

1 And He the witness gives
To loyal hearts and free,
That every promise is fulfilled,
If faith but brings the plea.

Rev. L. Hartsough.
Copyright.

COME, EVERY SOUL.
(Tune—G. H. 5o, No. 17o.)

1 Come, every soul by sin oppressed,
There's mercy with the Lord,
And He will surely give you rest,
By trusting in his word.

CHORUS.
Only trust Him, only trust Him,
Only trust Him now;
He will save you, He will save you,
He will save you now.

2 For Jesus shed His precious blood
Rich blessings to bestow;
Plunge now into the crimson flood
That washes white as snow.

178

Dr. J. J. MAXFIELD.

BY FAITH WE FOLLOW JESUS.

1. By faith we fol-low Je - sus, And how to His con - trol; We drink the liv-ing wa - ter
2. While pressing on we won - der, What yet this peace shall he; It flow - eth like a riv - er
3. The way is growing bright - er, As years are go - ing by; And we with clearer vis - ion
4. A few more years of wait-ing The dawn-ing of the day, And Christ will send His an-gels

So pre-cious to the soul; 'Tis bliss - ful on the moun-tain, And bless-ed in the vale!
That wid - ens to the sea! If storms around us gath - er, They bring a sweet-er calm;
Can see our home on high; Is this the land of Beu - lah Where sins no more go down?
To bear our souls a - way; Then we shall leave the val - ley Our wea - ry feet have trod,

Chorus.

The joy of trusting Je - sus, Is joy that cannot fail, Blest home beyond the Jor - dan.
For still the soul keeps singing, A more triumphant psalm.
While birds are sweetly singing, We press towards our crown.
To spend a long to-mor-row In rest and peace with God. Blest home beyond the Jor-dan.

Blest home beyond the Jor - dan.

By per. of W. A. Ogden, owner of Copyright.

BY FAITH WE FOLLOW JESUS.—Concluded.

Our home so bright and fair; Where we shall meet our lov'd ones That wait our coming there.

Our home so bright and fair; Where we shall meet our lov'd ones

177 PASS ME NOT.

(Tune G. H. 5—6, No. 164.)

1 Pass me not, O gentle Saviour,
  Hear my humble cry;
  While on others Thou art smiling,
  Do not pass me by.

CHORUS.

Saviour, Saviour,
  Hear my humble cry,
  While on others Thou art calling,
  Do not pass me by.

2 Trusting only in Thy merit,
  Would I seek Thy face;
  Heal my wounded, broken spirit,
  Save me by Thy grace.

Copyright.

178 THE PRECIOUS NAME.

(Tune G. H. 1—2, No. 47.)

1 Take the name of Jesus with you,
  Child of sorrow and of woe—
  It will joy and comfort give you,
  Take it, then, where'er you go.

CHORUS.

Precious name, O how sweet!
  Hope of earth and joy of heav'n;
  Precious name, O how sweet!
  Hope of earth and joy of heav'n.

2 O the precious name of Jesus!
  How it thrills our souls with joy,
  When His loving arms receive us,
  And His songs our tongues em-
       ploy.

Copyright.

179 EVERY DAY AND HOUR.

(Tune G. H. 1—2, No. 59.)

1 Saviour, more than life to me,
  I am clinging, clinging close to
       Thee;
  Let Thy precious blood applied
  Keep me ever, ever near Thy side.

REFRAIN.

Every day, every hour,
  Let me feel Thy cleansing power;
  May Thy tender love to me
  Bind me closer, closer, Lord, to
       Thee.

2 Let me love Thee more and more,
  Till this fleeting, fleeting life is
       o'er;
  Till my soul is lost in love,
  In a brighter, brighter world above.

Copyright.

THE SHEPHERD IS CALLING.

ALEXCENAH THOMAS.

W. A. OGDEN.

1. Jesus, the Shepherd is call-ing,
2. Even the children He's call-ing,
3. Come, while the Shepherd is pleading,

Wanderer, calling for thee;
They are the lambs of His fold;
Come, He is waiting to - day;

Here in His word, He in-vit-eth,
Tenderly now He'll receive them,
Now by His Spirit He's lead ing

Saying, oh, "Come unto me;"
As He once took them of old;
Lit tle ones in-to the way;

Ye who are weary, oh, hear Him;
E'en in His arms He will take them,
Leading them on like a Shepherd.

Ye who are la den with care;
Safe shall they rest in His love,
In - to the pastures of life.

Come, while the Shep-herd is call - ing,
And in His mer - cy He'll make them
Where they shall eat and ne'er hun - ger,

Come, and your bur - den He'll bear.
Heirs of His King dom a - bove.
Free from all sor - row and strife.

FINE.

D.S.—Je - sus, the Shep-herd is call - ing.   Ten - der - ly call - ing for thee.

Copyright, 1894, by W. A. Ogden. Used by per.

Refrain.

Call - ing for thee, ... ing for thee, ...

Call-ing for thee, He's call-ing for thee, for thee

Call - ing for thee, He's call-ing for thee.

191 TOPLADY, 7s.
(Tune—G. H. 5ed, No. 200)

1 Rock of Ages, cleft for me,
Let me hide myself in Thee;
Let the water and the blood,
From Thy wounded side which flowed.
Be of sin the double cure—
Save from wrath and make me pure.

2 Could my tears forever flow,
Could my zeal no languor know,
These for sin could not atone;
Thou must save, and Thou alone:
In my hand no price I bring;
Simply to Thy cross I cling.

A. M. Toplady.

192 BETHANY.
(Tune—G. H. 5ed, No. 223.)

1 Nearer, my God, to Thee,
Nearer to Thee!
E'en though it be a cross
That raiseth me;
Still all my song shall be.
Nearer, my God, to Thee,
Nearer to Thee!

2 Though, like a wanderer,
The sun gone down,
Darkness be over me,
My rest a stone;
Yet in my dreams I'd be
Nearer, my God, to Thee,
Nearer to Thee!

Sarah F. Adams.

193 HAPPY DAY.
(Tune—G. H. 5ed, No. 363.)

1 O happy day that fixed my choice
On Thee, my Saviour and my God;
Well may this glowing heart rejoice,
And tell its raptures all abroad.

Chorus.

Happy day, happy day,
When Jesus washed my sins away;
He taught me how to watch and pray,
And live rejoicing every day;
Happy day, happy day,
When Jesus washed my sins away.

2 Now rest, my long-divided heart:
Fixed on this blissful centre rest:
Nor ever from Thy Lord depart.
With Him of every good possessed.

Philip Doddridge.

182

BRING YE THE LILIES.

Neva E. Prentice.

N. K. Griggs.

1. O, O bring ye the lil-ies for His crown-ing, For the Lord is a-ris-en in-deed;
2. O, O bring ye the lil-ies as a tok - en Of the Lord who is ris-en in might:
3. O, O bring ye the lil-ies, pure and how - ly, As a sign of the peace He will give:

As a sym-bol of the face nev-er frown-ing, Of the Friend who is faith-ful in need.
And hath promised in His word, nev-er brok - en — We shall dwell with the an - gels of light.
As an emblem of His love pure and ho - ly, And a pledge of the life we shall live.

Chorus.

O, bring ye the lil-ies, bring ye the lil-ies, Bring ye the lil-ies for His crown'-ing.

From "The Lilies." By per.

BRING YE THE LILIES.—Concluded.

He's the fair-est of the fair, and the Friend we need; Praise ye the Lord! He is ris-en in-deed.

1165 SHALL WE MEET?

(Tune—G. H. 1st No. 108.)

1 Shall we meet beyond the river,
  Where the surges cease to roll?
  Where in all the bright forever,
  Sorrow ne'er shall press the soul?

Chorus.

Shall we meet, shall we meet,
Shall we meet, beyond the river?
Shall we meet beyond the river?
Where the surges cease to roll.

2 Shall we meet in that blest harbor
  When our stormy voyage is o'er?
  Shall we meet and cast the anchor
  By the fair, celestial shore?

3 Shall we meet in yonder city,
  Where the tow'rs of crystal
    shine?
  Where the walls are all of jasper,
  built by workmanship divine?

H. L. Hastings.

1166 OH, THINK OF THE HOME.

(Tune—G. H. 1st No. 54.)

1 Oh, think of the home over there,
  By the side of the river of light,
  Where the saints, all immortal
    and fair,   [white.
  Are robed in their garments of

Chorus.

Over there, over there,
Oh, think of the home over there,
Over there, over there, over there,
Oh, think of the home over there.

2 Oh, think of the friends over
    there,
  Who before us the journey have
    trod,
  Of the songs that they breathe
    on the air,
  In their home in the palace of
    God.

D. W. C. Huntington.

1167 GUIDE ME.

(Tune—G. H. 1st No. 12.)

1 Guide me, O Thou great Jehovah!
  Pilgrim thro' this barren land
  I am weak, but Thou art mighty,
  Hold me with Thy powerful hand.
    Bread of heaven,
  Feed me till I want no more.

2 Open now the crystal fountain,
  Whence the healing waters flow;
  Let the fiery, cloudy pillar
  Lead me all my journey thro';
    Strong Deliverer,
  Be Thou still my strength and
    shield.

3 When I tread the verge of Jordan,
  Bid my anxious fears subside;
  Bear me thro' the swelling current,
  Land me safe on Canaan's side;
    Songs of praises,
  I will ever give to Thee.

W. Williams.

GOD WILL TAKE CARE OF YOU.

FANNY J. CROSBY.

IRA D. SANKEY.

1. God will take care of you, be not a - fraid; He is your safeguard thro' sunshine and shade;
2. God will take care of you thro' all the day, Shielding your foot steps, di - rect - ing your way;
3. God will take care of you, long as you live, Grant-ing you bless-ings no oth - er can give.

Ten-der-ly watch-ing and keeping His own, He will not leave you to wan-der a - lone;
He is your Shep-herd, Pro-tec-tor and Guide, Lead-ing His chil-dren where still wa-ters glide.
He will take care of you when time is past, Safe to His king-dom will bring you at last.

Chorus.

God will take care of you still to the end; Oh, what a Fa - ther, Re-deem-er and Friend!

Copyright, 1900, by Ira D. Sankey.

GOD WILL TAKE CARE OF YOU.—Concluded.

Je - sus will an - swer when-ev - er you call,   He will take care   of you; trust Him for all.

1199   CORONATION.
(Tune—G. H. 5-6, No. 201.)

1 All hail the power of Jesus' name!
　Let angels prostrate fall;
　Bring forth the royal diadem,
　And crown Him Lord of all.

2 Ye chosen seed of Israel's race,
　Ye ransomed from the fall,
　Hail Him who saves you by His grace,
　And crown Him Lord of all.

3 Let every kindred, every tribe,
　On this terrestrial ball,
　To Him all majesty ascribe,
　And crown Him Lord of all.
　　　　　　　　　Edward Perronet.

200   LOVING KINDNESS.
(Tune—G. H. 5-6, No. 142.)

1 Awake, my soul, to joyful lays,
　And sing thy great Redeemer's praise;
　He justly claims a song from me;
　His loving kindness, O how free!

REFRAIN

His loving kindness, loving kindness,
His loving kindness, O how free!

2 He saw me ruined in the fall,
　Yet loved me notwithstanding all;
　And saved me from my lost estate:
　His loving kindness, O how great!

3 I often feel my sinful heart
　Prone from my Saviour to depart;
　But, though I oft have Him forgot,
　His loving kindness faileth not.
　　　　　　　　　S. Medley.

201   HAMBURG. L.M.
(Tune—G. H. 1-2, No. 7-2.)

1 Just as I am, without one plea,
　But that Thy blood was shed for me,
　And that Thou bidst me come to Thee,
　O Lamb of God! I come, I come.

2 Just as I am, and waiting not
　To rid my soul of one dark blot,
　To Thee, whose blood can cleanse each spot,
　O Lamb of God! I come, I come.

3 Just as I am, though tossed about
　With many a conflict, many a doubt,
　With fears within, with foes without,
　O Lamb of God! I come, I come.
　　　　　　　　　Charlotte Elliott.

186

GOD IS WITH US.

Dr. J. J. Maxfield.

W. A. Ogden.

1. Not a - lone, O bless - ed Je - sus; Thou hast shown our feet the way, And the cloud and fi - ry
2. Flee - ing from our cru - el bond - age, Pass we thro' the part - ed sea,
3. We may drink the bit - ter wa - ters, Where our desert Marahs flow. Or lie down to sleep at

pil - lar, Go be - fore us night and day. Darkness flies be - fore the promise. All our desert paths are
descrt—Draw us, Saviour, un - to Thee. Let the car - nal nature per - ish. Give the per - fect rest with -
Bethel, Where the an - gels come and go. But a - long the wea - ry marches, God will rain His man - na

light. Tho' we oft may pause at E - lim, (Canaan ris - es to our sight.)
in: Let the precious blood of Je - sus, (Cleanse us wholly from our sin.)
down: We may eat and live for - ev - er.—First the cross, and then the crown.)

*Chorus.

"The best of all is, God is

* Last words of John Wesley.

Used by per. of W. A. Ogden, owner of Copyright.

GOD IS WITH US.—Concluded.

with us," "Jesus reigns the ages through, Nations rise, decline and perish, God remains for-ev-er true.

204 WE SHALL MEET.

(Tune—G. H. 5-6, No. 188.)

1 We shall meet beyond the river,
   By and by, by and by;
   And the darkness will be over,
   By and by, by and by;
   With the toilsome journey done,
   And the glorious battle won,
   We shall shine forth as the sun,
   By and by, by and by.

2 We shall strike the harps of glory,
   By and by, by and by;
   We shall sing redemption's story,
   By and by, by and by;
   And the strains for evermore
   Shall resound in sweetness o'er
   Yonder everlasting shore;
   By and by, by and by.

John Atkinson. Copyright

203 MISSIONARY HYMN.

(Tune—G. H. 5-6, No. 237.)

1 From Greenland's icy mountains
   From India's coral strand,
   Where Afric's sunny fountains
   Roll down their golden sand—
   From many an ancient river,
   From many a palmy plain,
   They call us to deliver
   Their land from error's chain.

2 What though the spicy breezes
   Blow soft o'er Ceylon's isle;
   Though every prospect pleases,
   And only man is vile;
   In vain with lavish kindness
   The gifts of God are strewn;
   The heathen, in his blindness,
   Bows down to wood and stone.

R. Heber.

205 MORNING LIGHT.

(Tune—G. H. 5-6, No. 246.)

1 The morning light is breaking,
   The darkness disappears;
   The sons of earth are waking
   To penitential tears:
   Each breeze that sweeps the ocean
   Brings tidings from afar,
   Of nations in commotion,
   Prepared for Zion's war.

2 See heathen nations bending
   Before the God we love,
   And thousand hearts ascending
   In gratitude above;
   While sinners, now confessing,
   The gospel call obey,
   And seek the Saviour's blessing,
   A nation in a day.

Samuel F. Smith.

206 BRINGING IN THE SHEAVES.

(Tune—G. H. 5, No. 193.)

1 Sowing in the morning, sowing
  seeds of kindness,
Sowing in the noontide and the
  dewy eve;
Waiting for the harvest, and the
  time of reaping,
We shall come rejoicing, bring-
  ing in the sheaves.

Cho.— : Bringing in the sheaves,
  Bringing in the sheaves,
We shall come, rejoicing,
  Bringing in the sheaves.:

2 Sowing in the sunshine, sowing
  in the shadow,
Fearing neither clouds nor win-
  ter's chilling breeze;
By and by the harvest, and the la-
  bor ended,
We shall come, rejoicing, bring-
  ing in the sheaves.

                         Knowles Shaw.

207 MY FAITH LOOKS UP.

(Tune—G. H. 5, No. 229.)

1 My Faith looks up to Thee,
  Thou Lamb of Calvary,
    Saviour divine!
  Now hear me while I pray,
  Take all my guilt away,
  O let me from this day
    Be wholly Thine.

2 May Thy rich grace impart
Strength to my fainting heart,
    My zeal inspire;
  As Thou hast died for me,
  O may my love to Thee,
  Pure, warm, and changeless be,
    A living fire.

                         Ray Palmer.

208 JESUS IS CALLING.

(Tune—G. H. 5, No. 42.)

1 Jesus is tenderly calling thee home—
  Calling to-day, calling to-day;
  Why from the sunshine of love
    wilt thou roam
  Farther and farther away?

REFRAIN.

Calling to-day, calling to-day,
Jesus is calling, is tenderly calling
  to-day.

2 Jesus is calling the weary to rest—
  Calling to-day, calling to-day;
  Bring Him thy burden, and thou
    shalt be blest;
  He will not turn thee away.

3 Jesus is waiting, oh! come to Him
    now—
  Waiting to-day, waiting to-day;
  Come with thy sins, at His feet
    lowly bow;
  Come, and no longer delay.

                         Fanny J. Crosby.

Copyright.

209 DRAW ME NEARER.

(Tune—G. H. 5, No. 156.)

1 I am Thine, O Lord, I have heard
    Thy voice,
  And it told Thy love to me;
  But I long to rise in the arms of
    faith,
  And be closer drawn to Thee.

REFRAIN.

Draw me nearer, nearer, blessed
  Lord,   [died]
  To the cross where Thou hast
  Draw me nearer, nearer, nearer,
    blessed Lord,
  To Thy precious, bleeding side.

2 There are depths of love that I
    cannot know
  Till I cross the narrow sea;
  There are heights of joy that I
    may not reach
  Till I rest in peace with Thee.

                         Fanny J. Crosby.

Copyright.

210 THE OLD, OLD STORY.

(Tune—G. H, C., No. 27.)

1 Tell me the Old, Old Story
  Of unseen things above,
  Of Jesus and His glory,
  Of Jesus and His love.
  Tell me the story simply,
    As to a little child,
  For I am weak and weary,
  And helpless and defiled.

REFRAIN.

Tell me the Old, Old Story,
Tell me the Old, Old Story,
Tell me the Old, Old Story,
  Of Jesus and His love.

2 Tell me the same Old Story,
  When you have cause to fear
  That this world's empty glory
    Is costing me too dear;
  Yes, and when that world's glory
    Is dawning on my soul,
  Tell me the Old, Old Story:
    "Christ Jesus makes thee whole."
                         Kate Hankey.

211 DOXOLOGY.

Praise God, from all blessings flow,
Praise Him all creatures here below:
Praise Him above, ye heavenly host:
Praise Father, Son, and Holy Ghost.
                         Bishop Ken.

INDEX OF SUBJECTS.

The numbers indicate pages.

INDEX.

Titles in SMALL CAPS: First lines in Roman.

(The Figures refer to the Page.)

Index.

www.ingramcontent.com/pod-product-compliance
Lightning Source LLC
Chambersburg PA
CBHW030837270326
41928CB00007B/1102